LIFE IN EARNEST.

SIX LECTURES,

ON

CHRISTIAN ACTIVITY AND ARDOR.

BY THE REV. JAMES HAMILTON,

AUTHOR OF "HARP ON THE WILLOWS," ETC.

NOT SLOTHFUL IN BUSINESS;
FERVENT IN SPIRIT;
SERVING THE LORD.
Rom. xii. 11

NEW YORK:
ROBERT CARTER & BROTHERS
285 BROADWAY.

1853.

CONTENTS.

TO THE

KIRK-SESSION AND CONGREGATION

OF THE

NATIONAL SCOTCH CHURCH,

REGENT SQUARE.

My dear Friends:—

It sometimes adds to the interest, and even to the usefulness of a book, to know the reason of its publication. I may therefore mention in the outset, that it is for your sakes that the following pages appear in print. As all my efforts can not secure that amount of pastoral intercourse for which I long, I felt desirous of sending to your several homes a word in season at the opening of this year; and, as an appropriate remembrancer at such a time, I have selected the following familiar lectures. You now receive them in nearly the same homely guise in which you first made their acquaintance a few sabbaths ago.* For the directness of the style and the plainness of the illustrations, I do not apologize. They are not more a natural propensity than the result of conscientious conviction;† for as I can not be persuaded that, in matters of taste, anything is eloquent which does not answer the end in view, nor that in theolo-

* They were delivered as part of a course of lectures on the Romans, on the morning and evening of sabbaths, November 17 and 24, and December 1, 1844. Except the fourth, of which there were no written notes, they appear with few retrenchments or alterations.

† 2 Cor. iii. 12; Matt. xiii. 3.

gy anything is sublime which is not scriptural: so I can not think that, in preaching, anything is out of place which puts the truth in its proper place—in the memories and the hearts of the hearers—nor that anything is mean which can trace its pedigree back to the Mount of Beatitudes. But while I offer no apology for the style of these lectures, I tender my cordial thanks to those hearers whose earnestness, or intellectual elevation, or personal kindness, has made them listen so willingly to a mode of preaching not the less distasteful because it can plead exalted precedents; and I own that it has been not the least comfort of my ministry, that among yourselves, preaching like the following specimen has found so many attentive hearers. There is only one satisfaction greater—the belief that many are applying practically what most hear so patiently.

And now, dear brethren, were it not the restraining thought that colder eyes than yours may look upon these pages, there are many things I would like to say. I would like to commemorate some of the mercies which have crowned the three and a half years during which we have worshipped together; and I would like to give you some idea of my own affection for you. To the elders for counsel never asked nor adopted in vain—to both elders and deacons for days and portions of the night devoted to labors of love, which but for their pains-taking could never have been accomplished—to the self-denying teachers of the sabbath-school and of the week-evening class—and to all who have contributed their willing aid in various schemes of usefulness—I would tender a pastor's warmest gratitude. And I would like to mention with gratitude to God two things which have made my own heart often glad—the harmony of our church, and the happiness of your abodes. Wherever I see innocent or holy joy, I try to make some of it my own; and I believe that most of my earthly happiness of late has been a transfusion from your joy. Seldom does a day transpire without seeing as much in-door comfort and tranquillity—as much mutual affection of heads of families, and parents and children, and brothers and sisters—with so evident an aspect of God's blessing on many homes, as are an unspeakable delight to me. Does not God's goodness in this respect often strike yourselves, and make you sing the twenty-third psalm?

> "My table thou hast furnished
> In presence of my foes;
> My head thou dost with oil anoint,
> And my cup overflows.
>
> "Goodness and mercy all my life
> Shall surely follow me:
> And in God's house for evermore
> My dwelling-place shall be."

And in some measure the result of domestic piety and peace, I here record with gratitude our congregational harmony. Sure enough we have hitherto dwelt together in unity ; and as I can truly say for my brethren, your office-bearers, that our anxiety is your edification, so has your "order" been our "joy."

But while the acknowledgment of God's goodness is the delightful employment of a closing year, it is no less incumbent, with an opening year, to consider what more we can do for the God of our mercies in the days or months to come. As a church, we have congregational duties, and each member of the church has personal duties. Let your minister remind you of some of these.

1. Let this new year be a year of greater *activity*. Be diligent in your proper calling, in seeking personal improvement, and in doing good. Ply your daily calling in a

Christian spirit, doing nothing by constraint or grudgingly, but adorning the doctrine of God your Savior by your patient, sprightly, and thoroughgoing industry. Seek personal improvement. Give yourselves to the reading of instructive and religious books; and when friends meet, let them strive to give the conversation a profitable turn, and one which may minister to the use of edifying. The Young Men's Society is an incentive to study, and an outlet for the results of reading; and those young men who are desirous of mutual improvement should all be members of it. Engage in some direct effort to do good. An earnest and willing spirit will find or make a field of usefulness for itself. Ascertaining, in the course of their visits to the poor, that in many families the older girls could read little or none, and were kept at home during the day, attending to the younger children, a few ladies opened a class at five in the afternoon, to teach these girls to read and write, and undertook to conduct it personally. In a short time the room was full, and there are now about seventy of these young people learning to read the Word of God intelligently, who, but for this self-denying experiment, must have grown up in ignorance. We know of similar efforts on a less extended scale. And in the same spirit, several local prayer-meetings have been opened, and are attended by people not likely to have found their way to any other place of worship. The diligence of district visiters has been productive of much obvious benefit in bringing several back to the forsaken sanctuary, and the affectionate assiduity of the sabbath-school teachers has in several hopeful instances reaped its present reward. Brethren, be ambitious of doing good. Seek to leave the world the better for your sojourn in it. Whatever you attempt, endeavor to do it so thoroughly, and follow it up so resolutely, that the result shall be ascertained and evident. And in your attempts at usefulness, be not only conscientious but enthusiastic. Love the work. Redeem the time. Remember that the Lord is at hand.

2. Let this new year be a year of greater *liberality*. There are some objects to which of late you have given very largely; and there are those among you who give to every object freely, and with a self-denying generosity. But by a little systematic forethought and contrivance, begun now and carried through the year, many might double their contributions without at all abridging their real enjoyments. The maxim "I can do without it"—if all Regent Square acted on it for a single year, might build a school or send out a missionary. If all the

money which you children spend on cakes and toys, and which we grown-up people spend on playthings and parties, were put into the Lord's treasury, we should have as much as we wanted for all our congregational purposes, and a great deal over to help our neighbors. And while some are striving how much they can *do*, let others strive how much they can *give* to the cause of Christ this year. Those who excel in the one are likely to excel in the other; fo. just as those who have too little faith to give, have usually too little fervor to work, so the hardest workers are usually the largest givers.

3. Let this be a year of greater *spirituality*. As the holy Joseph Alleine wrote from Ilchester prison to his flock at Taunton, "Beloved Christians, live like yourselves; let the world see that the promises of God, and privileges of the gospel, are not

empty sounds, or a mere crack. Let the heavenly cheerfulness, and the restless diligence, and the holy raisedness of your conversations, prove the reality, and excellency, and beauty of your religion to the world." Aim at an elevated life. Seek to live so near to God, that you shall not be overwhelmed by those amazing sorrows which you may soon encounter, nor surprised by that disease which may come upon you in a moment, suddenly. Let prayer never be a form. Always realize it as an approach to the living God for some specific purpose; and learn to watch for the returns of prayer. Let the Word of God dwell in you richly. That sleep will be sweet and that awaking hallowed where a text of Scripture, or a stanza of a spiritual song, imbues the last thoughts of consciousness. Occasionally read the biography of some eminent Christian, such as Doddridge, or Pearce, or Martyn, or Fletcher, or Charles of Bala, or R. M'Cheyne : for it will show how much of Christ's presence may be enjoyed here on earth, and may stir you up to a more loving, devout, and watchful life. Do not forsake any of the stated assemblies for worship ; and let friends, when they meet, often converse on those things which may edify one another. See that you make progress ; see that when the year is closing, you have not all the evil tempers and infirmities of character which presently afflict you ; but see to it that if God grant you to sit down on the Ebenezer of another closing year, you may be able to look back on radiant spots where you enjoyed seasons of spiritual refreshing and victories over enemies heretofore too strong for you. Happy new year! if its path were so bright and its progress so vivid, that in a future retrospect your eye could fix on many a Bethel and Peniel along its track, and your grateful memory could say, "Yonder is the grave where I buried a long-besetting sin, and that stone of memorial marks where God made me to triumph over a fierce temptation through Jesus Christ. Yon sabbath was the top of the hill where I clasped the cross, and the burden fell off my back; and that communion was the land of Beulah, where I saw the far-off land and the king in his beauty."

"Come, let us anew our journey pursue,
Roll round with the year,
And never stand still till the Master appear.

"His adorable will let us gladly fulfil,
And our talents improve,
By the patience of hope and the labor of love

"O that each in the day of his coming may say,
'I have fought my way through;
I have finished the work thou didst give me to do.'

"O that each from his Lord may receive the glad word,
'Well and faithfully done:
Enter into my joy, and sit down on my throne.'"

My dear friends, it is a blessed thing to know the Savior—to feel that your soul is safe. You have been in a ship when it entered the harbor, and you have noticed the different looks of the passengers as they turned their eyes ashore. There was one who, that he might not lose a moment's time, had got everything ready for landing long ago; and now he smiles and beckons to yon party on the pier, who, in their turn, are so eager to meet him, that they almost press over the margin of the quay: and no sooner is the gangway thrown across, than he has hold of the arm of one, and another is triumphant on his shoulder, and all the rest are leaping before and after him on their homeward way. But there was another who showed no alacrity. He gazed with pensive eye on the nearer coast, and seemed to grudge that the trip was over. He was a stranger, going among strangers;

and though sometimes during the voyage he had a silent hope that something unexpected might occur, and that some friendly face might recognise him in regions where he was going an alien and an adventurer—no such welcoming face is there ; and with reluctant steps he quits the vessel, and commits himself to the unknown country. And now that every one else has disembarked, who is this unhappy man whom they have brought on deck, and, groaning in his heavy chains, whom they are conducting to the dreaded shore ? Alas ! he is a felon and a runaway, whom they are bringing back to take his trial there : and no wonder he is loath to land.

Now, dear brethren, our ship is sailing fast. We shall soon hear the rasping on the shallows, and the commotion overhead, which bespeak the port in view. When it comes to that, how shall you feel ? Are you a stranger, or a convict, or are you going home? Can you say, "I know whom I have believed?" Have you a Friend within the veil? And however much you may enjoy the voyage, and however much you may like your fellow-passengers, does your heart sometimes leap up at the prospect of seeing Jesus as he is, and so being ever with the Lord?

The Lord send you a happy, a holy, and a useful year! Accept this little token of your pastor's wish to help your faith and joy; and believe me

Your ever-affectionate minister,

JAMES HAMILTON.

January 1, 1845.

LIFE IN EARNEST.

LECTURE I.

INDUSTRY.

'*Not slothful in business.*"—ROMANS XII. 11.

Two things are very certain—that we have all got a work to do, and are all, more or less, indisposed to do it: in other words, every man has a calling, and most men have a greater or less amount of indolence, which disinclines them for the work of that calling. Many men would have liked the gospel all the better, if it had entirely repealed the sentence, "In the sweat of thy brow shalt thou eat thy bread;" had it proclaimed a final emancipation from industry, and turned our world into a merry playground or luxurious dormitory. But this is not what the gospel does. It does not abolish labor; it gives it a new and a nobler aspect. The gospel abolishes labor much in the same way as it abolishes death: it leaves the thing, but changes its nature. The gospel sweetens the believer's work: it gives him new motives for performing it. The gospel dignifies toil; it transforms it from the drudgery of the workhouse or the penitentiary to the affectionate offices and joyful services of the fireside and the family circle. It asks us to do for the sake of Christ many things which we were once compelled to bear as a portion of the curse, and which worldly men perform for selfish and secondary reasons. "Whatsoever ye do in word or deed, do all in the name of the Lord Jesus. Wives, submit yourselves unto your own husbands, as it is fit in the Lord. Children, obey your parents in all things, for this is well-pleasing unto the Lord. Servants, obey in all things your masters according to the flesh, not with eye-service, as men-pleasers, but in singleness of heart, fearing God; and whatsoever ye do, do it heartily as to the Lord and not unto men, knowing that of the Lord ye shall receive the reward of the inheritance, for ye serve the Lord Christ." The gospel has not superseded diligence. "Study to be quiet and to do your own business, and to work with your own hands, as we commanded you. If any man will not work, neither let him eat." It is mentioned as almost the climax of sin—"And withal they learn to be idle, wandering about from house to house; and not only idle, but tattlers also, and busy-bodies, speaking things which they ought not:" as, on the other hand, the healthy and right-conditioned state of a soul is—"Not slothful in business, fervent in spirit, serving the Lord."

I. This precept is violated by those who have no business at all. By the bounty of God's providence, some are in such a situation, that they do not ne[illegible] to toil for a subsistence; they go to bed when they please, and get up when they can sleep no longer, and they do with themselves whatever they like; and though we dare not say that theirs is the happiest life, it certainly is the easiest. But it will neither be a lawful life nor a happy one, unless it have some work in hand, some end in view. Those of you who are familiar with the shore, may have seen attached to the inundated reef a creature—whether a plant or animal you could scarcely tell—rooted to the rock as a plant might be, and twirling its long tentacula as an animal would do. This plant-animal's life is somewhat monotonous, for it has nothing to do but grow and twirl its feelers, float in the tide, or fold itself up on its foot-stalk when that tide has receded, for months and years together. Now, would it not be very dismal to be transformed into a zoophyte? Would it not be an awful punishment, with your human soul still in you, to be anchored to a rock, able to do nothing but spin about your arms or fold them up again, and knowing no variety, except when the receding ocean left you in the daylight, or the returning waters plunged you into the green depths again, or the sweeping tide brought you the prize of a young periwinkle or an invisible star-fish ? But what better is the life you are spontaneously leading ? What greater variety marks your existence, than chequers the life of the sea-anemone ? Does not one day float over you after another, just as the tide floats over it, and find you much the same, and leave you vegetating still ? Are you more useful ? What real service to others did you render yesterday ? What tangible amount of occupation did you overtake in the one hundred and sixty-eight hours of which last week consisted ? And what higher end in living have you than that polypus ? You go through certain mechanical routines of rising, and dressing, and visiting, and dining, and going to sleep again ; and are a little roused from your usual lethargy by the arrival of a friend, or the effort needed to write some note of ceremony. But as it courtesies in the waves, and vibrates its exploring arms, and gorges some dainty medusa, the sea-anemone goes through nearly the same round of pursuits and enjoyments with your intelligent and immortal self. Is this a life for a rational and responsible creature to lead?

II. But this precept is also violated by those who are diligent in trifles—whose activity is a busy idleness. You may be very earnest in a pursuit which is utterly beneath your prerogative as an intelligent creature, and your high destination as an immortal being. Pursuits which are perfectly proper in creatures destitute of reason, may be very culpable in those who not only have reason, but are capable of enjoyments above the range of reason itself. We this instant imagined a man retaining all his consciousness transformed into a zoophyte. Let us imagine another similar transformation : fancy that instead of a polypus you were changed into a swallow. There you have a creature abundantly busy, up in the early morning, for ever on the wing, as graceful and sprightly in his flight as tasteful in the haunts which he selects. Look at him, zigzagging over the clover-field, skimming the limpid lake, whisking round the steeple, or dancing gayly in the sky. Behold him in high spirits, shrieking out his ecstasy as he has bolted a dragon-fly, or darted through the arrow-slits of the old turret, or performed some other feat of hirundine agility. And notice how he pays his morning visits—alighting elegantly on some housetop, and twittering politely by turns to the swallow on either side of him, and after five minutes' conversation, off and away to call for his friend at the castle. And now he is gone upon his travels—gone to spend the winter at Rome or Naples, to visit Egypt or the Holy Land, or perform some more *recherché* pilgrimage to Spain or the coast of Barbary. And when he comes home next April, sure enough he has been abroad: charming climate—highly delighted with the cicadas in Italy, and the bees on Hymettus —locusts in Africa rather scarce this season; but, upon the whole, much pleased with his trip, and returned in high health and spirits. Now, dear friends, this is a very proper life for a swallow, but is it a life for you? To flit about from house to house; to pay futile visits, where, if the talk were written down, it would amount to little more than the chattering of a swallow; to bestow all your thoughts on graceful attitudes, and nimble movements, and polished attire; to roam from land to land, with so little information in your head, or so little taste for the sublime or beautiful in your soul, that could a swallow publish his travels, and did you publish yours, we should probably find the one a counterpart of the other: the winged traveller enlarging on the discomforts of his nest, and the wingless one on the miseries of his hotel or his château; you describing the places of amusement, or enlarging on the vastness of the country, and the abundance of the game, and your rival eloquent on the self-same things. Oh! it is a thought—not ridiculous, but appalling. If the earthly history of some of our brethren were written down; if a faithful record were kept of the way they spend their time; if all the hours of idle vacancy or idler occupancy were put together, and the very small amount of useful diligence deducted, the life of a bird or quadruped would be a nobler one—more worthy of its powers and more equal to its Creator's end in forming it. Such a register is kept. Though the trifler does not chronicle his own vain words and wasted hours, they chronicle themselves. They find their indelible place in that book of remembrance with which human hand can not tamper, and from which no erasure save one can blot them. They are noted in the memory of God. And when once this life of wondrous opportunities and awful advantages is over—when the twenty or fifty years of probation are fled away—when mortal existence, with its facilities for personal improvement and serviceableness to others, is gone beyond recall—when the trifler looks back to the long pilgrimage, with all the doors of hope and doors of usefulness, past which he skipped in his frisky forgetfulness—what anguish will it move to think that he has gambolled through such a world without salvation to himself, without any real benefit to his brethren, a busy trifler, a vivacious idler, a clever fool!

III. Those violate this precept who have a lawful calling, a proper business, but are slothful in it. When people are in business for themselves, they are in less risk of transgressing this injunction, though even there it sometimes happens that the hand is not diligent enough to make its owner rich. But it is when engaged in business, not for ourselves, but for others, or for God, that we are in greatest danger of neglecting this rule. The servant who has no pleasure in his work, who does no more than wages can buy, or a legal agreement enforce; the shopman who does not enter *con amore* into his employer's interest, and bestir himself to extend *his* trade as he would strive were the concern his own; the scholar who trifles when his teacher's eye is elsewhere, and who is content if he can only learn enough to escape disgrace; the teacher who is satisfied if he can only convey a decent quantum of instruction, and who does not labor for the mental expansion and spiritual well-being of his pupils, as he would for those of his own children; the magistrate or civic functionary who is only careful to escape public censure, and who does not labor to make the community richer, or happier, or better, for his administration; the minister who can give his energies to another cause than the cause of Christ, and neglect his Master's business in minding his own; every one, in short, who performs the work which God or his brethren have given him to do in a hireling and perfunctory manner, is a violator of the Divine injunction, "Not slothful in business." There are some persons of a dull and languid turn. They trail sluggishly through life, as if some painful viscus, some adhesive slime, were clogging every movement, and making their snail-path a waste of their very substance. They do nothing with that healthy alacrity, that gleesome energy, which bespeaks a sound mind even more than a vigorous body; but they drag themselves to the inevitable task with remonstrating reluctance, as if every joint were set in a socket of torture, or as if they expected the quick flesh to cleave to the next implement of industry they handled. Having no wholesome love to work, no joyous delight in duty, they do everything grudgingly, in the most superficial manner, and at the latest moment. Others there are, who, if you find them at their post, you will find them dozing at it. They are a sort of perpetual somnambulists, walking through their sleep; moving in a constant mystery; looking for their faculties, and forgetting what they are looking for; not able to find their work, and when they have found their work, not able to find their hands; doing everything dreamily, and therefore everything confusedly and incompletely; their work a dream, their sleep a dream, not repose, not refreshment, but a slumberous vision of rest, a dreamy query concerning sleep; too late for everything, taking their passage when the ship has sailed, insuring their property when the house is burnt, locking the door when the goods are stolen—men whose bodies seem to have started in the race of existence before their minds were ready, and who are always gazing out vacantly as if they expected their wits were coming up by the next arrival. But, besides the sloths and the somnambulists, there is a third class—the day-dreamers. These are a very mournful, because a self-deceiving generation. Like a man who has his windows glazed with yellow glass, and who can fancy a golden sunshine, or a mellow autumn on the fields, even when a wintry sleet is sweeping over them, the day-dreamer lives in an elysium of his own creating. With a foot on either side of the fire—with his chin on his bosom, and the wrong end of the book turned toward him—he can pursue his self-complacent musings till he imagines himself a traveller in unknown lands—the explorer of Central Africa—the solver of all the unsolved problems in science—the author of some unprecedented poem at which the wide world is wondering—or something so stupendous that he even begins to quail at his own glory. The misery is, that while nothing is done toward attaining the greatness, his luxurious imagination takes its possession for granted: and with his feet on the fender, he fancies himself already on the highest pinnacle of fame; and a still greater misery is, that the time thus wasted in unprofitable musings, if spent in honest application and down right working, would go very far to carry him where his sublime imagination fain would be. It would not be easy to estimate the good of which day-dreams have defrauded the world. Some of the finest intellects have exhaled away in this sluggish evaporation, and left no vestige on earth except the dried froth, the obscure film, which survives the drivel of vanished dreams; and others have done just enough to show how important they would have been had they awaked sooner or kept longer awake at once. Sir James Macintosh was an example of the latter class. His castle-building "never amounted to conviction; in other words, these fancies have never influenced my actions; but I must confess that they have often been as steady and of as regular recurrence as conviction itself, and that they have sometimes created a little faint expectation, a state of mind in which my wonder that they should be realized would not be so great as it rationally ought to be."* Perhaps no one in modern times has been capable of more sagacious or comprehensive generalizations in those sciences which hold court in the high places of human intellect than he; but a few hints and a fragment of finished work are all that remain. Coleridge never sufficiently woke up from

* Life, vol. i., p. 5.

his long life-dream to articulate distinctly any of the glorious visions which floated before his majestic fancy, some of which we really believe that the world would have been the wiser for knowing. And, returning from secular philosophy to matters of Christian practice, has the reader never met those whose superior gifts would have made them eminently useful, and who had designs of usefulness, perhaps philanthropic schemes of peculiar ingenuity and beauty, but who are passing away from earth, if they have not passed away already, without actually attempting any tangible good? And yet so sincere are they in their own inoperative benevolence, so hard do they toil and sweat in their own Nephelococcygia, that nothing could surprise them more than the question, "What do ye more than others?" unless it were their own inability to point out the solid product, and lay their hands on the actual results. To avoid this guilt and wretchedness—

1. Have a business in which diligence is

lawful and desirable. There are some pursuits which do not deserve to be called a business. Æropus was the king of Macedonia, and it was his favorite pursuit to make lanterns.* Probably he was very good at making them, but his proper business was to be a king; and therefore the more lanterns he made, the worse king he was. And if your work be a high calling, you must not dissipate your energies on trifles—on things which, lawful in themselves, are still as irrelevant to you as lamp-making is irrelevant to a king. Perhaps some here are without any specific calling. They have neither a farm nor a merchandise to look after; they have no household to care for, no children to train and educate, no official duties to engross their time; they have an independent fortune, and live at large. My friends, I congratulate you on your wealth, your

* Quoted in Todd's Student's Guide (chap. v.)—a book which no zealous student will read without being animated by its vigorous tone, and instructed by its wise and practical suggestions.

liberal education, your position in society, and your abundant leisure. It is in your power to be the benefactors of your generation; you are in circumstances to do an eminent service for God and finish some great work before your going hence. What that work shall be, I do not attempt to indicate; I rather leave it for your own investigation and discovery. Every one has his own line of things. Howard chose one path, and Wilberforce another; Harlan Page chose one, and Brainerd Tailor another. Mrs. Fletcher did one work, Lady Glenorchy another, and Mary Jane Graham a third. Every one did the work for which God had best fitted them, but each made that work their *business*. They gave themselves to it; they not only did it, by-the-by, but they selected it and set themselves in earnest to it, not parenthetically, but on very purpose—the problem of their lives—for Christ's sake and in Christ's service, and held themselves as bound to do it as if they had been by himself expressly engaged for it. And, brethren, you must do the same. Those of you who do not need to toil for your daily bread, your very leisure is a hint what the Lord would have you to do. As you have no business of your own, he would have you devote yourselves to *his* business ; he would have you carry on, in some of its manifold departments, that work which he came to earth to do. He would have you go about his Father's business as he was wont to be about it. And if you still persist in living to yourselves, you can not be happy. You can not spend all your days in making pin-cushions, or reading newspapers, or loitering in club-rooms and coffee-houses, and yet be happy. If you profess to follow Christ, this is not a Christian life. It is not a conscientious, and so it can not be a comfortable life. And if the pin-cushion or the newspaper fail to make you happy, remember the reason—very good as relaxations, ever so great an amount of these things can never be a *business*, and "wist ye not that you should be about your Father's business?"

2. Having made a wise and deliberate selection of a business, go on with it—go through with it. Persevering mediocrity is much more respectable, and unspeakably more useful, than talented inconstancy. In the heathery turf you will often find a plant chiefly remarkable for its peculiar roots: from the main stem down to the minutest fibre, you will find them all abruptly terminate as if shorn or bitten off; and the silly superstition of the country people alleges that once on a time it was a plant of singular potency for healing all sorts of maladies, and therefore the great enemy of man in his malignity bit off the roots in which its virtues resided. This plant, with this quaint history, is a very good emblem of many well-meaning but little-effecting people. They might be defined as *radicibus præmorsis*, or rather *inceptis succisis*. The efficacy of every good work lies in its completion: and all their good works terminate abruptly, and are left off unfinished. The devil frustrates their efficacy by cutting off

their ends; their unprofitable history is made up of plans and projects, schemes of usefulness that were never gone about, and magnificent undertakings that were never carried forward; societies that were set agoing, then left to shift for themselves, and forlorn beings who for a time were taken up and instructed, and just when they were beginning to show symptoms of improvement, were cast on the world again. But others there are, who, before beginning to build, count the cost, and having collected their materials, and laid their foundations deep and broad, go on to rear their structure, indifferent to more tempting schemes and sublime enterprises subsequently suggested. The man who provides a home for a poor neighbor, is a greater benefactor of the poor than he who lays the foundation of a stately almshouse and never finishes a single apartment. The persevering teacher who guides one child into the saving knowledge of Christ and leads him on to established habits of piety, is a more useful man than his friend

4*

who gathers in a room-full of ragged children, and after a few weeks of waning zeal, turns them all adrift on the streets again. The patriot who set his heart on abolishing the slave-trade, and after twenty years of rebuffs and revilings, of tantalized hope and disappointed effort, at last succeeded—achieved a greater work than if he had set afloat all possible schemes of philanthropy, and then left them, one after the other, to sink or swim. So short is life, that we can afford to lose none of it in abortive undertakings; and once we are assured that a given work is one which it is worth our while to do, it is true wisdom to set about it instantly, and once we have begun it, it is true economy to finish it.

LECTURE II.

INDUSTRY.

"*Not slothful in business.*"—ROMANS XII. 11.

THIS morning we saw how this precept is violated by various descriptions of persons: by those who have no business at all, and those whose business is only an active idleness: and, finally, by those who, having a lawful business—a good and honorable work assigned them—do it reluctantly or drowsily, or leave it altogether undone.

There are some who have no business at all. They are of no use in the world; they are doing no good, and attempting none; and when they are taken out of the world, their removal creates no vacancy. When an oak or any noble and useful tree is uprooted, his removal creates a blank. For years after, when you look to the place which once knew him, you see that something is missing. The branches of adjacent trees have not yet supplied the void. They still hesitate to occupy the place formerly filled by their powerful neighbor; and there is still a deep chasm in the ground—a rugged pit—which shows how far his giant roots once spread. But when a leafless pole, a wooden pin, is plucked up, it comes easy and clean away. There is no rending of the turf, no marring of the landscape, no vacuity created, no regret. It leaves no memento, and is never missed. Now, brethren, which are you? Are you cedars, planted in the house of the Lord, casting a cool and grateful shadow on those around you? Are you palm-trees, fat and flourishing, yielding bounteous fruit, and making all who know you bless you? Are you so useful, that, were you once away, it would not be easy to fill your place again : but people, as they pointed to the void in the plantation—the pit in the ground—would say, "It was here that that brave cedar grew : it was here that that old palm-tree diffused his familiar shadow and showered his mellow clusters?" Or are you a peg—a pin—a rootless, branchless, fruitless thing that may be pulled up any day, and no one ever care to ask what has become of it? What are you doing? What are you contributing to the world's happiness, or the church's glory? What is your *business?*

Individuals there are who are doing something, though it would be difficult to specify what. They are busy; but it is a busy idleness.

"Their only labor is to kill the time,
And labor dire it is, and weary wo.
They sit, they loll, turn o'er some idle rhyme,
Or saunter forth, with tottering steps and slow:
This soon too rude an exercise they find—
Straight on the couch their limbs again they throw,
Where hours on hours they sighing lie reclined,
And court the vapory god soft-breathing in the wind."—*Castle of Indolence.*

They think that they are busy, though their chief business be to get quit of themselves. To annihilate time, to quiet conscience, to banish care, to keep *ennui* out at one door, and serious thoughts out at the other, gives them all their occupation. And, betwixt their fluttering visits and frivolous engagements, their midnight diversions, their haggard mornings, and shortened days, their yawning attempts at reading, and sulky application to matters of business which they can not well evade; betwixt mobs of callers and shoals of ceremonious notes, they fuss and fret themselves into the pleasant belief that they are the most worried and hard-driven of mortal men. Even when groaning in prospect of interminable hours they have not a moment to spare; and a chief employment of their leisure is to appear in a constant hurry. Could you embody in matter-of-fact all their sham activity and bustling show, could you write down a truthful enumeration of the doings of a single week, I fear there would not be found one act which, were He saying, "Thou fool, this night shall thy soul be required of thee," the Judge of all would accept as a right deed or rightly done. It is possible to be very busy, and yet very idle. It is possible to be serious about trifles, and to exhaust one's energies in doing nothing. It is possible to be toiling all one's days in doing that which, in the infatution of fashion or the delirium of ambition, will look exceedingly august and important; but which the first flash of eternity will transmute into shame and everlasting contempt.

Then, among those who have really got a work to do—whose calling is lawful or something more—perhaps a direct vocation in the service of God, there are three classes who violate the precept of the text—those who do their work grudgingly, or drowsily, or not at all—the sloths, the somnambulists, and the day-dreamers. Some do it grudgingly. They have not a heart for work; and of all work, least heart for that which

God has given them. Instead of that angelic alacrity which speeds instinctively on the service God assigns, that healthy love of labor which a loyal and well-conditioned soul would have, they postpone everything to the latest moment, and then go whimpering and growling to the hated task as if they were about to undergo some dismal punishment. They have a strange idea of occupation. They look on it as a drug, a penalty, a goblin, a fiend, something very fierce and cruel, something very nauseous; and they would gladly smuggle through existence by one of those side-paths which the grim giants, labor and industry, do not guard.

Others again, who do not quite refuse their work, put only half a soul into it. They have no zeal for their profession. They somehow scramble through it; but it is without any noble enthusiasm—any appetite for work or any love to the God who gives it. If they are intrusted with the property of others, they can not boast as

Jacob did: "In the day the drought consumed me, and the frost by night; and my sleep departed from mine eyes. God hath seen mine affliction and the labor of my hands." If intrusted with the souls of others, they can not reckon up "the abundant labors, the often journeyings, the weariness and painfulness, the watchings, the hunger and thirst," the perils and privations which, for the love of his Master and his Master's work, the Apostle of the Gentiles joyfully encountered. If scholars, they are content to learn the lesson, so that no fault shall be found. If servants, they aspire to nothing more than fulfilling their inevitable toils. And if occupying official stations, they are satisfied with a decent discharge of customary duties, and are glad if they leave things no worse than they found them. They are hireling, perfunctory, heartless in all they do. Their work is so sleepily done that it is enough to make you lethargic to labor in their company; and, before they go zealously and wakefully to work, they would need to be startled up into the daylight of actual existence—they would need to be shaken from that torpor into which the very sight of labor is apt to entrance them. Oh, happier far, to lose health and life itself in clear, brisk, conscious working; to spend the last atom of strength, and yield the vital spark itself in joyful wakeful efforts for Him who did all for us—than to drawl through a dreaming life, with all the fatigue of labor and nothing of its sweetness; snoring in a constant lethargy, sleeping while you work, and nightmared with labor when you really sleep.

And, besides the procrastinating and perfunctory class, those are "slothful in business" who do no business at all. And there are such persons—agreeable, self-complacent, plausible persons—who really fancy that they have done a great deal because they have intended to do so much. Their life is made up of good purposes, splendid projects, and heroic resolutions. They live in the region which the poet has described:—

"A pleasing land of drowsy-head it was,
Of dreams that wave before the half-shut eye,
And of gay castles in the clouds that pass,
For ever flushing round a summer's sky."

They have performed so many journeys, and made so many discoveries, and won so many laurels in this aërial clime, that life is over, and they find their real work is not begun. Like the dreamer who is getting great sums of money in his sleep, and who, when he awakes, opens his till or his pocket-book, almost expecting to find it full, the day-dreamer, the projector awaking up at the close of life, can hardly believe that after his distinct and glorious visions, he is leaving the world no wiser, mankind no richer, and his own home no happier, for all the golden prospects which have flitted through his busy brain. What a blessed world it were, how happy and how rich, if all the idlers were working, if all the workers were awake, and if all the projectors were practical men!

I trust, my friends, that many among

you are desirous to be active Christians. Perhaps the following hints may be helpful to those who wish to serve the Lord by diligence in business.

1. Have a calling in which it is worth while to be busy. There are many callings in which it is lawful for the Christian to "abide." He may be a lawyer like Sir Matthew Hale, or a physician like Haller, Heberden, and Mason Goode. He may be a painter like West, or a sculptor like Bacon, or a poet like Milton, and Klopstock, and Cowper. He may be a trader like Thornton and the Hardcastles, or a philosopher like Boyle and Boerhaave. He may be a hard-working artisan like the Yorkshire Blacksmith and the Watchmaker of Geneva; or he may toil for his daily bread like the Happy Waterman, and the Wallsend Miner, and the Shepherd of Salisbury Plain, and many a domestic servant of humble but pious memory. And the business of this ordinary calling, the disciple of Christ must discharge heartily,

and with all his might. He must labor to be eminent and exemplary in his own profession. He should seek, for the sake of the Gospel, to be *first-rate* in his own department. But over and above his ordinary calling as a member of society, the believer has his special calling as a member of the church. He has a direct work to do in his Savior's service. Some who now hear me have so much of their time at their own disposal, that they might almost make their calling as members of Christ's church the business of their lives. And each who is in this privileged situation should consider what is the particular line of things for which his taste and talents most urgently predispose him, and for which his training and station best adapt him. The healthiest condition of the church is where there is a member for every office, and where every member fulfils his own office,* where there are no defects and no transpositions, but each is allowed to ply to the utmost the

* Rom. xii. 3–8.

work for which God has intended him; where Newton writes his letters, and Butler his analogy; where in the leisure of the olden ministry, Matthew Henry compiles his commentary, and where in the calm retreat of Olney, Cowper pours forth his devotional melodies; where Venn cultivates his corner of the vineyard, and Whitefield ranges over the field of the world; where President Edwards is locked up in his study, and Wilberforce is detained in the parlor; where the adventurous Carey goes down into the pit, and the sturdy arm of Fuller deals out the rope; where he who ministers waits on his ministering, and he that teacheth on teaching, and he that exhorteth on exhortation, and he who hath to give gives liberally, and he who has method and good management rules diligently, and he who can pay visits of mercy pays them cheerfully. And if the Lord has given you an abundance of unoccupied leisure, he has along with it given you some talent or other, and says, "Occupy till I come."

Find out what it is that you best can do, or what it is which, if you neglect it, is likely to be left undone. And whether you select as your sphere of Christian usefulness, a sabbath class or a ragged school, a local prayer-meeting, or a district for domiciliary visitation; whether you devote yourself to the interests of some evangelistic society, or labor secretly from house to house, whatever line of things you select, make it your "business." Pursue it so earnestly, that though it were only in that one field of activity you would evince yourself no common Christian.

2. Make the most of TIME. Some have little leisure, but there are sundry expedients, any one of which, if fairly tried, would make that little leisure longer. (1.) *Economy.* Most of the men who have died enormously rich, acquired their wealth, not in huge windfalls, but by minute and careful accumulations. It was not one vast sum bequeathed to them after another, which overwhelmed them with inevitable

opulence; but it was the loose money which most men would lavish away, the little sums which many would not deem worth looking after, the pennies and half-crowns of which you would keep no reckoning, these are the items which year by year piled up, have reared their pyramid of fortune. From these money-makers let us learn the nobler "avarice of time." A German critic could repeat the Iliad in Greek. How many weeks did he bestow on the task of committing it to memory? He had no weeks to spare for such a purpose, for he was a physician in busy practice; but he contrived to master it all during the brief snatches of time when passing from one patient's door to another.* In the life of Dr. Mason Good, a feat of similar industry

* A similar instance of literary industry is recorded of Dr. Burney, the musician. With the help of pocket grammars and dictionaries, which he had taken the trouble to write out for his own use, he acquired the French and Italian languages when riding on horseback from place to place to give his professional instructions.

is recorded. "His translation of Lucretius was composed in the streets of London, during his extensive walks to visit his numerous patients. His practice was to take in his pocket two or three leaves of an octavo edition of the original; to read over a passage two or three times as he walked along, until he had engraven it upon his ready memory; then to translate the passage, meditate upon the translation, correct and elaborate it, until he had satisfied himself." Proceeding in the same way with a second, a third, and fourth passage, he entered the translation on his manuscript, after he had returned home, and disposed of all his professional business. And in order to achieve some good work which you have much at heart, you may not be able to secure an entire week, or even an uninterrupted day. But try what you can make of the broken fragments of time. Glean up its golden dust; those raspings and parings of precious duration, those leavings of days and remnants of hours which so many sweep out into the waste of existence. Perhaps, if you be a miser of moments, if you be frugal and hoard up odd minutes, and half-hours, and unexpected holydays, your careful gleanings may eke out a long and useful life, and you may die at last richer in existence than multitudes whose time is all their own. The time which some men waste in superfluous slumber, and idle visits, and desultory application, were it all redeemed, would give them wealth of leisure, and enable them to execute undertakings for which they deem a less worried life than theirs essential. When a person says, "I have no time to pray, no time to read the Bible, no time to improve my mind, nor to do a kind turn to a neighbor," he may be saying what he thinks, but he should not think what he says; for if he has not got the time already, he may get it by *redeeming* it. (2.) *Punctuality*. A singular mischance has occurred to some of our friends. At the instant when he ushered them on existence, God gave them a work to do, and he also gave them a competency of time, so much time, that, if they began at the right moment, and wrought with sufficient vigor, their time and their work would end together. But a good many years ago a strange misfortune befell them. A fragment of their allotted time was lost. They can not tell what became of it, but sure enough it has dropped out of existence; for, just like two measuring-lines laid alongside, the one an inch shorter than the other, their work and their time run parallel, but the work is always ten minutes in advance of the time. They are not irregular. They are never too soon. Their letters are posted the very minute after the mail is shut; they arrive at the wharf just in time to see the steamboat off; they come in sight of the terminus precisely as the station-gates are closing. They do not break any engagement nor neglect any duty; but they systematically go about it too late, and usually too late by about the same fatal interval. How can they retrieve the lost fragment, so essential to character and comfort? Perhaps by a device like this: suppose that on some auspicious morning they contrived to rise a quarter of an hour before their usual time, and were ready for their morning worship fifteen minutes sooner than they have been for the last ten years; or, what will equally answer the end, suppose that for once they merged their morning meal altogether, and went straight out to the engagements of the day; suppose that they arrived at the class-room, or the work-shop, or the place of business, fifteen minutes before their natural time, or that they forced themselves to the appointed rendezvous on the week-day, or to the sanctuary on the sabbath-day, a quarter of an hour before their instinctive time of going, all would yet be well. This system carried out would bring the world and themselves to synchronize; they and the marching hours would come to keep step again, and moving on in harmony, they would escape the jolting awkwardness and fatigue they used to feel, when old Father Time put the right foot foremost and they advanced the left; their reputation would be retrieved, and friends who at present fret would begin to smile; their fortunes would be made; their satisfaction in their work would be doubled; and their influence over others, and their power for usefulness would be unspeakably augmented. (3.) *Method.* A man has got twenty or thirty letters and packets to carry to their several destinations; but instead of arranging them beforehand, and putting all addressed to the same locality in a separate parcel, he crams the whole into his promiscuous bag, and trudges off to the West End, for he knows that he has got a letter directed thither: that letter he delivers, and hies away to the City, when lo! the same handful which brings out the invoice for Cheapside, contains a brief for the Temple, and a parliamentary petition, which should have been left, had he noticed it earlier, at Belgrave Square; accordingly he retraces his steps and repairs the omission, and then performs a transit from Paddington to Bethnal Green—till in two days he overtakes the work of one, and travels fifty miles to accomplish as much as a man of method would have managed in fifteen. The man who has thoroughly mastered that lesson—"A place for everything, and everything in its own place"—will save a world of time. He loses no leisure seeking for the unanswered letter or the lost receipt; he does not need to travel the same road twice; and hence it is that some of the busiest men have the least of a busy look. Instead of slamming doors, and ringing alarm-bells, and knocking over chairs and children in their headlong hurry, they move about deliberately, for they have made their calculations, and know that they have ample time. And just as a prodigal of large fortune is obliged to do shabby things, while an orderly man of moderate income has always an easy look, as if there were still something left in his pocket—as he can afford to pay for goods when he buys them, and to put something into the collecting-box when it passes him, and after he has discharged all his debts has still something to spare—so is it with the methodical husbanders and the disorderly spendthrifts of time. Those who live without a plan have never any leisure, for their work is never done : those who *time* their engagements, and arrange their work beforehand, can bear an occasional interruption. They can reserve an evening hour for their families ; they can sometimes take a walk into the country, or drop in to see a friend ; they can now and then contrive to read a useful book ; and amid all their important avocations, they have a tranquil and opulent appearance, as if they still had plenty of time. (4.) *Promptitude.* Every scene of occupation is haunted by that "thief of time," procrastination ; and all his ingenuity is directed to steal that best of opportunities, the present time. The disease of humanity, disinclination to the work God has given, more frequently takes the form of dilatoriness than a downright and decided refusal. But delay shortens life and abridges industry, just as promptitude enlarges both. You have a certain amount of work before you, and in all likelihood some unexpected engagements may be superadded as the time wears on. You may begin that work immediately, or you may postpone it till the evening, or till the week be closing, or till near the close of life. Your sense of duty insists on its being done; but procrastination says, "It will be pleasanter to do it by-and-by." What infatuation! to end each day in a hurry, and life itself in a panic! and when the flurried evening has closed, and the fevered life is over, to leave half your work undone! Whatever the business be, do it instantly, if you would do it easily: life will be long enough for the work assigned, if you be prompt enough. Clear off arrears of neglected duty; and once the disheartening accumulations of the past are overtaken, let not that mountain of difficulty rise again. Prefer duty to diversion, and cultivate that athletic frame of soul which rejoices in abundant occupation ; and you will soon find the sweetness of that repose which follows finished work, and the zest of that recreation in which no delinquent feeling mingles, and on which no neglected duty frowns.

LECTURE III.

AN EYE TO THE LORD JESUS.

"*Serving the Lord.*"—ROMANS XII. 11.

"SERVING the Lord." The title which James and Jude take to themselves at the outset of their epistles is, "James—Jude—a servant of Jesus Christ." The original is more forcible still. In the inscriptions of these epistles, as well as in this passage, a true and emphatic rendering would be, "a slave of Jesus Christ;"—"Not slothful in business, fervent in spirit, the Lord's *bond-men.*" The believer is the happy captive of Jesus Christ; he has fastened on himself

Immanuel's easy yoke, the light burden and delicious chains of a Savior's love; and though Christ says, "Henceforth I call you no more servants," the disciple can not give up the designation; there is no other term by which, at times, he can express that feeling of intense devotedness and self-surrender which fills his loyal bosom. "Truly, O Lord, I am thy servant, and the son of thy handmaid." And far from feeling any ignominy in the appellation, there are times when no name of Jesus sounds sweeter in his ear than "Jesus, my Lord! Jesus, my Master!" and when no designation more accords with his feeling of entire devotedness, than James, a servant, Jude, a slave of Jesus Christ, David, a bondsman of the Lord. There are times when the believer has such adoring views of his Savior's excellency, and such affecting views of his Savior's claims, that rather than refuse one requirement, he only grudges that the yoke is so easy that he can scarcely perceive it, the burden so light that he can scarcely recognise himself as a servant. He would like something which would identify him more closely with his beloved Savior, some open badge that he might carry, and which would say for him—

"I'm not ashamed to own my Lord."

If Christ would bore his ear to the door post—if Christ would only give him out of his own hand his daily task to do—he would like it well; and ceasing to be the servant of men, he would fain become the servant of Jesus Christ.

And going to the Savior in this ardent mood of mind, and saying, "Lord, what wouldst thou have me to do?" the Savior hands you back the Bible. He accepts you for his servant, and he directs you what service he would have you to perform. The book which he gives you is as really the directory of Christ's servants as is the sealed paper of instructions which the commander of an expedition takes with him when he goes to sea, or the letter of directions which the absent nobleman sends to the steward on his estates or the servant in his house. The only difference is, its generality. Instead of making out a separate copy for your specific use, indicating the different things which he would have you do from day to day, and sending it direct to yourself, authenticated by his own autograph, and by the precision and individuality of its details, evidently designed for yourself exclusively—the volume of his will is of a wider aspect and more miscellaneous character. It effectually anticipates each step of your individual history, and prescribes each act of your personal duty; but intermingling these with matters of promiscuous import, it leaves abundant scope for your honesty and ingenuity to find out the precise things which your Lord would have *you* to do. Had it been otherwise—had there been put into the hand of each disciple, the moment he professed his faith in Christ, a sealed paper of instructions, containing an enumeration of the special services which his Lord would have this new disciple to render, prescribing a certain number of tasks which he expected that disciple to perform, and specifying the very way in which he would have them done—in proportion as this directory was precise and rigid, so would it cease to be the test of fidelity, so would it abridge the limits within which an unrestricted loyalty may display itself. As it is, the directory is so plain, that he who runs may read: not so plain, however, but that he who stands still and ponders will find a great deal which the runner could not read. It is so peremptory, that no man can call Jesus Lord without doing the things which it commands; but withal so general, as to leave many things to the candor and cordiality of sound-hearted disciples. It is precise enough to indicate the tempers, and the graces, and the good works, with which the Savior is well pleased, and by which the Father is glorified; but it nowhere fixes the exact amount of any one of these, short of which Christ will not suffer a disciple to stop, or beyond which he does not expect a disciple to go. The Bible does not deal in maximums and minimums; it does not weigh and measure out by definite proportions the ingredients of regenerate character; but it specifies what these ingredients are, and leaves it to the zeal of each believer to add to his faith, not *as many*, but *as much of each* of these things as he pleases. Firmly averring, on the one hand, that without each and all of these graces a man can not belong to Christ, it, on the other hand, omits to specify how much of each a man must be able to produce before Jesus say to him, "Well done, good and faithful servant; enter thou into the joy of thy Lord." The Bible announces those qualities which a man must have, in order to prove him born from above; but it does not tell what quantity of each he must exhibit, in order to secure the smile of his Master, and an abundant entrance into his heavenly kingdom. By this definiteness on the outward side, it leaves no room for hypocrisy; but, by this indefiniteness on the inner side, it leaves large place for the works, and service, and faith, and patience—the filial enterprise, the affectionate voluntaries, and free-will offerings—of those who know no limit to their labors, except the limit of their love to Christ.

You will observe, that at the time when you become a disciple of Christ, your Lord and Master takes the whole domain of your employments under his own jurisdiction. He requires you to consecrate your ordinary calling to him, and to do, over and above, many special things expressly for himself. Whatsoever you do, in word or deed, he desires that you should do it in his name: not working like a worldling, and praying like a Christian, but both in work and prayer, both in things secular and things sacred, setting himself before you, carrying out his rules, and seeking to please him. One is your Master, even Christ, and he is your master in everything—the master of your thoughts, your words, your family arrangements, your business transactions—the master of your working time, as well as of your sabbath-day—the Lord of your shop and counting-room, as well as of your closet and your pew—because the Lord of your affections, the proprietor of your very self besides. The Christian is one who may do many things from secondary motives—from the pleasure they afford his friends—from the gratification they give to his own tastes and predilections—from his abstract convictions of what is honest, lovely, and of good report; but his main and predominant motive—that which is paramount over every other, and which, when fully presented, is conclusive against every other—is affection for his heavenly Friend. One is his Master, even Christ, and the love of Christ constraineth him.

Look now at the advantages of a motive like this. See how loyalty to Christ secures diligence in business—whether that be business strictly religious or business more miscellaneous.

1. Love to Christ is an abiding motive. It is neither a fancy, nor a sentiment, nor an evanescent emotion. It is a *principle*—calm, steady, undecaying. It was once a problem in mechanics to find a pendulum which should be equally long in all weathers—which should make the same number of vibrations in the summer's heat and in the winter's cold. They have now found it out. By a process of compensations they make the rod lengthen one way as much as it contracts another, so that the centre of motion is always the same: the pendulum swings the same number of beats in a day of January as in a day of June; and the index travels over the dial-plate with the same uniformity, whether the heat try to lengthen or the cold to shorten the propelling power. Now the moving power in some men's minds is sadly susceptible of surrounding influences. It is not principle, but feeling, which forms their pendulum-rod; and according as this very variable material is affected, their index creeps or gallops, they are swift

or slow in the work given them to do. But principle is like the compensation-rod, which neither lengthens in the languid heat, nor shortens in the brisker cold ; but does the same work day by day, whether the ice-winds whistle, or the simoom glows. Of all principles, a high-principled affection to the Savior is the steadiest and most secure. Other incentives to action are apt to alter or lose their influence altogether. You once did many things for the sake of friends whose wishes expressed or understood were your incentive, and whose ready smile was your recompense. But that source of activity is closed. Those friends are now gone where your industry can not enrich them, nor your kindness comfort them. Or if they remain, they are no longer the same that once they were. The magic light has faded from off them. The mysterious interest which hovered round them has gone up like a mountain-mist, and left them in their wintry coldness or natural ruggedness : no longer those whom once you took them to be Or you did many things for fame; and were well requited for a winter's work when the hosanna of a tumultuous assembly, or the pæan of a newspaper paragraph, proclaimed you the hero of the hour. But even that sort of satisfaction has passed away, and, meager diet as these plaudits always were, you stand on the hungry pinnacle, and, like other aspirants of the same desert-roaming school * you snuff; but, alas! the breeze has changed. The popular taste, the wind of fashion, has entirely veered about; and, except an occasional tantalizing whiff from the oasis of a receding popularity, the sweet gust of its green pastures regales you no more. Or you used to work for money—for literal bank-notes and pieces of minted metal; yes, mere money was your motive. And you would sit up till midnight, or rise in the drowsy morning, to get one piece more. And so truly was this money your chief end—"Where the treasure is, there will the heart be also"—do you not feel as if

* Jeremiah xiv. 6.

your money-safe were the metropolis of your affections? Where your money is, is not your heart there also? Were your fortune to clap its wings and fly away, would not you feel as if your happiness had fled away? Have not your very thoughts got a golden tinge?—and, tracing some of this sabbath's meditations back to their source, would you not soon land in the till, the exchange, the counting-room? Is not gold your chiefest joy? But have not flashes of truth from time to time dismayed you?—"What am I living for? For a make-believe like this? for a glittering cheat which (in the way that I am using it) will be forgotten in heaven or felt like a canker in hell? How shall I wake up my demented self from this spell-dream, and seek some surer bliss, some more enduring joy? For grant that I shall be buried in a coffin of gold, and commemorated in a diamond shrine, what the happier will it make the *me* that then shall be?" And even without these brighter convictions, without these momentary eaks in the general delirium of covetousness, do you not feel a duller dissatisfaction occasionally creeping over you and paralyzing your busy efforts? "Well—is this right? This headlong hunt of fortune, is it the end for which my Creator sent me into the world? Is it the highest end for which my immortal self can live? Is it the best way of bestowing that single sojourn in this probation-world which God has given me? And what am I the better? Am I sure that I myself am the happier for it? Dare I flatter myself that, in bequeathing so much money, I bequeath to my children consolidated happiness, a sure and certain good, an inevitable blessing?" And such intrusive thoughts, whose shadows, at least, flit across most serious minds, are very damping to effort—very deadening to diligence in business. Merely serving your friends—in mere pursuit of fame—merely seeking a fortune—you are in constant danger of having all motive annihilated, and so all effort paralyzed. But whatever be the business in hand—from the veriest trifle up to the sublimest enterprise—from binding a shoe-latchet to preparing a highway for the Lord—if only you be conscious that this is the work which HE has given you to do, you can go on with a cheerful serenity and strenuous satisfaction, for you will never want a motive. And it is just when other motives are relaxing into languor, that the compensation we spoke of comes into play ; and the constraining love of Christ restores the soul and keeps its rate of activity quick and constant as ever. The love of Christ is an abiding motive, and can only lose its power where reason has lost its place. No man ever set the Lord before him and made it his supreme concern to please his Master in heaven, yet lived to say, " What a fool am I ! What a wasted life is mine ! What vanity and vexation has Christ's service been ! Had I only my career to begin anew, I would seek another master and a higher end."* The Lord Jesus ever lives, and

* See Life of Rev. Henry Venn, under A. D. 1785.

never changes; and therefore the believer's love to his Savior never dies. Growing acquaintance may bring out new aspects of his character; but it will never disclose a reason why the believing soul should love him less than it loved at first. Growing acquaintance will only divulge new reasons for exclaiming, "Worthy is the Lamb!" and fresh motives for living, not unto ourselves, but unto Him that loved us and gave himself for us.

2. Love to Christ is a motive equal to all emergencies. There is a ruling passion in every mind; and when every other consideration has lost its power, this ruling passion retains its influence. When they were probing among his shattered ribs for the fatal bullet, the French veteran exclaimed, "A little deeper, and you will find the emperor." The deepest affection in a believing soul is the love of its Savior. Deeper than the love of home—deeper than the love of kindred, deeper than the love of rest and recreation, deeper than the love of life—is

the love of Jesus. And so, when other spells have lost their magic, when no name of old endearment, no voice of onwaiting tenderness, can disperse the lethargy of dissolution, the name that is above every name, pronounced by one who knows it, will kindle its last animation in the eye of death. And when other persuasives have lost their power, when other loves no longer constrain the Christian, when the love of country no longer constrains his patriotism, nor the love of his brethren his philanthropy, nor the love of home his fatherly affection—the love of Christ will still constrain his loyalty. There is a love to Jesus which nothing can destroy. There is a leal-heartedness which refuses to let a much-loved Savior go, even when the palsied arm of affection is no longer conscious of the benignant form it embraces. There is a love, which amid the old and weary "feel" of waning years renews its youth, and amid outward misery and inward desolation preserves its immortal root; which even when the glassy eye of hunger has forgot to sparkle, and the joy at the heart can no longer mantle on the withered cheek, still holds on, faithful to Jesus, though the flesh be faint. This was the love which made Paul and Silas, fatigued and famished as they were, and sleepless with pain, sing praise so loud that their fellow-prisoners heard and wondered. This was the love which burned in the apostle's breast, even when buffeting the Adriatic's wintry brine, and made the work which at Rome awaited him beam like a star of hope through the drowning darkness of that dismal night. This was the love which thawed his pen, when the moan of wintry winds made him miss the cloak he left at Troas, and impelled him to write to Timothy a testamentary entreaty to "hold fast" the truths which were hastening himself to martyrdom. Devotedness to Christ is a principle which never dies, and neither does the diligence which springs from it.

Dear brethren, get love to the Lord Jesus, and you have everything. Union to

Jesus is salvation. Love tc Jesus is religion. Love to the Lord Jesus is essential and vital Christianity. It is the mainspring of the life of God in the soul of man. It is the all-inclusive germe, which involves within it every other grace. It is the pervasive spirit, without which the most correct demeanor is but dead works, and the seemliest exertions are an elegant futility. Love to Christ is the best incentive to action—the best antidote to idolatry. It adorns the labors which it animates, and hallows the friendships which it overshadows. It is the smell of the ivory wardrobe—the precious perfume of the believer's character—the fragrant mystery which only lingers round those souls which have been to a better clime. Its operation is most marvellous; for when there is enough of it, it makes the timid bold, and the slothful diligent. It puts eloquence into the stammering tongue, and energy into the withered arm, and ingenuity into the dull, lethargic brain. It takes possession of the soul, and a joyous lustre beams in languid eyes, and wings of new obedience sprout from lazy, leaden feet. Love to Christ is the soul's true heroism, which courts gigantic feats, which selects the heaviest loads and the hardest toils, which glories in tribulations, and hugs reproaches, and smiles at death till the king of terrors smiles again. It is the aliment which feeds assurance—the opiate which lulls suspicions—the oblivious draught which scatters misery, and remembers poverty no more. Love to Jesus is the beauty of the believing soul; it is the elasticity of the willing steps, and the brightness of the glowing countenance. If you would be a happy, a holy, and a useful Christian, you must be an eminently Christ-loving disciple. If you have no love to Jesus at all, then you are none of his. But if you have a little love—ever so little—a little drop, almost frozen in the coldness of your icy heart—oh! seek more. Look to Jesus, and cry for the Spirit till you find your love increasing; till you find it drowning besetting sins; till you find it drowning guilty fears—rising, till it touch that index, and open your closed lips—rising, till every nook and cranny of the soul is filled with it, and all the actions of life and relations of earth are pervaded by it—rising, till it swell up to the brim, and, like the apostle's love, rush over in a full assurance: "Yes, I am persuaded, that neither death, nor life, nor angels, nor principalities, nor powers, nor things present, nor things to come, nor height, nor depth, nor any other creature, shall be able to separate us from the love of God, which is in Christ Jesus our Lord."

LECTURE IV.

A FERVENT SPIRIT.

"*Fervent in spirit.*"—ROMANS XII. 11.

THE description of work which a man performs will depend very much on the master whom he serves; but, the amount and quality of that work will depend as much on the mood of mind in which he does it. The master may be good, and the things which he commands may be good; but unless the servant have an eager, willing mind, little work may be done, and that little may not be well done. This is the glory of the gospel. It not only invites you to be the disciples of a Savior, whose requirements are as worthy of your most strenuous obedience as he himself is worthy of your warmest love, but it undertakes to give you the energy and enterprise which the service of such a master demands. Besides assigning a good and honorable work for your "business," and Him whom principalities and powers adore for your master, the gospel offers you the zealous mind which such a work requires, and which such a master loves.

But what is a fervent spirit?

1. It is a believing spirit. Few men have faith. There are few to whom the Word of God is solid, to whom "the things hoped for" are substantial, or "the things unseen" evident. There are few who regard the Lord Jesus as living now, or as taking a real and affectionate charge of his people here on earth. There are few who yet expect to see him, and who are laying their account with standing before his great white throne. But the believer has got an open

eye. He has looked within the veil. He knows that the things seen are temporal, and the things unseen are eternal. He knows that the Lord Jesus lives, and that though unseen, he is ever near. He may often forget, but he never doubts his promise: "And lo! I am with you always." This assurance of his ascending Savior, every time he recalls it, infuses alacrity, animation, earnestness. The faith of this is fervor. "Yes, blessed Savior! art thou present now? and seest thou thy disciple trifling thus? Is the book of remembrance filling up, and are these idle words and wasted hours my memorial there? And art thou coming quickly and bringing thy reward, to give each servant as his work shall be? And is this my 'work?' Lord, help my unbelief. Dispel my drowsiness. Supplant my sloth, and perfect thy strength in me."

2. A fervent spirit is an affectionate spirit. It is one which cries Abba, Father. It is full of confidence and love. Peter had a

fervent spirit, but it would be hard to say whether most of his fervor flowed through the outlet of adoration or activity. You remember with what a burst of praise his first epistle begins, and how soon he passes on to practical matters. "Blessed be the God and Father of our Lord Jesus Christ, which according to his abundant mercy, hath begotten us again unto a lively hope by the resurrection of Jesus Christ from the dead, to an inheritance incorruptible and undefiled, and that fadeth not away."—"Wherefore laying aside all malice, and all guile and hypocrisies, and all evil speakings, as newborn babes, desire the sincere milk of the word, that ye may grow thereby."—"Likewise, ye wives, be in subjection to your own husbands."—"The elders which are among you I exhort, who am also an elder."* And as in his epistle, so in his living character. His full heart put force and promptitude into every movement. Is his master encompassed by fierce ruffians? Peter's ar-

* 1 Peter, commencement of chapters i., ii., iii., v.

dor flashes in his ready sword, and converts the Galilean boatman into the soldier instantaneous. Is there a rumor of a resurrection from Joseph's tomb? John's nimbler foot distances his older friend, but Peter's eagerness outruns the serener love of John, and past the gazing disciple he bolts breathless into the vacant sepulchre. Is the risen Savior on the strand? His comrades secure the net, and turn the vessel's head for shore; but Peter plunges over the vessel's side, and, struggling through the waves, in his dripping coat falls down at his Master's feet. Does Jesus say, "Bring of the fish ye have caught?" Ere any one could anticipate the word, Peter's brawny arm is lugging the weltering net with its glittering spoil ashore; and every eager movement unwittingly is answering beforehand the question of his Lord, "Simon, lovest thou me?" And that fervor is the best, which, like Peter's, and as occasion requires, can ascend in ecstatic ascriptions of adoration and praise, or follow Christ to prison and to death; which can concentrate itself on feats of heroic devotion, or distribute itself in the affectionate assiduities of a miscellaneous industry.

3. A fervent spirit is a healthy spirit. When a strong spring gushes up in a stagnant pool, it makes some commotion at the first; and looking at the murky stream with its flotilla of duckweed tumbling down the declivity, and the expatriated newts and horse-leeches crawling through the grass; and inhaling the miasma from the inky runnel, you may question whether the irruption of this powerful current has made matters any better. But come anon, when the living water has floated out the stagnant elements, and when, instead of mephitic mud skimmed over with a film of treacherous verdure, the bright fountain gladdens its mirrored edge with its leaping fulness, then trips away on its merry path, the benefactor of thirsty beasts and weary fields. So the first manifestations of the new and the spiritual element in a carnal mind are of a mingled

sort. The pellicle of decency, the floating duckweed of surface-seemliness, which once spread over the character, is broken up, and accomplishments, and amusing qualities—which made the man very companionable and agreeable—have for the present disappeared. There is a great break-up ; and it is the passing away of the old things, which is at first more conspicuous and less pleasing, than the appearance of the new. In these earlier stages of regenerate history, the contrition and self-reproach of the penitent often assume the form of an artificial demureness and voluntary humility ; and in the general disturbance of those elements which have long lain in their specious stagnation, defects of character formerly hidden are perceived sooner than the beauties of a holiness scarce yet developed. But "Spring up, O well ! sing ye unto it." If this incursive process go freely on—if the living water spring up fast enough to clear out the sedimentary selfishness of the natural mind, with its reptile inmates—if the inflowings of heavenly life be copious enough to impart a truly "fervent spirit"*—come again. Survey that character when the love of God has become its second nature. In place of the silt and evil savor, the mean and sordid motives which once fermented there, view the simplicity and godly sincerity, the light-welcoming transparency, which reflects the Sun of Righteousness above it and the forms of truth around it; and instead of the fast-evaporating scantiness of its former selfishness, follow its track of diffusive freshness through the green pastures which it gladdens, and beneath those branches which gratefully sing over it.† Like a sweet fountain, a fervent spirit is beneficent; its very health is healing; its peace with God and joy from God are doing constant good; the gospel of its smiling aspect impresses strangers and comforts saints. And besides this unconscious and incidental usefulness,

* Compare the original, τω πνευματι ζεοντες, with John iv. 14, and vii. 38, 39.

† Psalm civ. 10, 12.

its active outpourings are a benefit as wide as its waters run. A Christian who is both active and fervent is doing perpetual good, and good in the most benignant way. The substantial service he does is doubly blessed by the joyful, loving, and hopeful spirit in which he does it; and though it were only by the gladness which skirts its course, and the amenities which bloom wherever it overflows, beholders might judge how "living," how life-awakening that water is, which Jesus gives to them that believe in him.

The best, the healthiest, is that calm and constant fervor we have now described; but just as there are intermitting springs which take long time to fill, and then exhaust their fulness in a single overflow—and as there are geysers which jet their vociferous waters high in air, and then are silent for long together—so there are Christians who do not lack fervor, but it comes in fits. They are intermitting springs; they take long to fill, and are emptied in a single gush. Or they are geysers. Some years ago they went up in an explosion of zeal—a smoking whirl-spout of fervor—but all is cold and silent now. The water is living, but the well is peculiar; it is only periodically filled; it seldom overflows. But just as you would not like to depend on an intermitting fountain for your cup of daily water, nor to owe the irrigation of your fields to the precarious bounty of a boiling spring—as the well near which you pitch your tent, or build your house, is the Elim whose bulging fulness invites you to plunge your pitcher at any hour, and whose deep-fed copiousness is constantly wimpling off in fertilizing streams—so you may be happy to perceive the incidental usefulness even of that zeal which comes fitfully; but you would select as the benefactor of the church, and as your own resort, the full heart to which you never can come wrong, and whose perennial redundance bespeaks a secret feeding from the river which makes glad the city of our God.

4. A fervent spirit is a happy spirit.—

Health is happiness. Peace with God is the life of the soul, and joy in God is its health. That assured and elevated believer who enjoys everything in God and God in everything, must needs be fervent. His inward blessedness makes him bountiful, and to do good and to communicate are things which, in his happy mood of mind, he can not help. Some Christians are too dejected. They got under the covert of a peculiar theology, or ensconce themselves in shadowy caves of wilfulness, or pertinacity, or unbelief; and then complain that they can not see the Sun of Righteousness. He lightens the world.* Let them come out beneath his beams, and at once they will feel the fire. Their shivering faith, which with them is rather the reminiscence of heat, than a resorting to its unfailing source, will soon mount up to fervor. To look to Jesus is to come to God, and to come home to God is to be happy. An estranged or suspicious spirit can not be fervent. Then

* John i. 9.

some Christians are not fervent because they are cumbered with so many things. They carry all their own burdens, and from their sympathizing disposition they have charged themselves with many burdens of their brethren also ; but instead of devolving these personal and relative solicitudes on an all-suffering Savior, they carry the whole melancholy load themselves. A fearful or a fretful spirit can not be fervent ; but there is no need for a believer in Jesus to be troubled or afraid.* Let him deposite all his anxieties in that Ear which is gracious enough to attend to the most trivial, and leave them in that Hand which is mighty enough to disperse the most tremendous ; and relieved of this incubus, his spirit will acquire an elasticity equal to the most arduous or most multifarious toils. And some believers are not sufficiently fervent, from being straitened in themselves. They do not open their souls to those felicitating influences with which a God of love surrounds them

* John xiv. 1.

on every side. There is as much comfort in the Word of God, and as mnch beauty in his works, and as much kindness in his dispensations, as, admitted into the soul, would inundate it with ecstasy. But many hearts are perverse; they let gloomy thoughts and bitter fancies flow freely in, and are almost jealous lest a drop of strong consolation should trickle through on this deluge of Marah. Brethren, it depends on which floodgate you open, whether you be drowned in a tide of joy or of sorrow. It depends on whether your well-springs are above or beneath, whether your consolation or your grief abounds. If you listen to what the Amen, the Faithful Witness, is saying,* and what God the Father is saying,† and what the Spirit and the Bride are saying,‡ and what a glorious universe is saying,|| and what the gracious events in your daily history are saying,§ your murmurings will sub-

* John xiv.–xvi. † Matt. iii. 17.
‡ Rev. xxii. 17. || Ps. viii., xix., civ.
§ Ps. cvii. Isaiah xxxviii. 19. Gen. xxxv. 3.

side into silence, and your vexing thoughts will be drowned in gratitude. Think much of God's chief mercy, and take thankful note of his lesser gifts. And when you have put on this girdle of gladness, your glory will sing and your gratitude will dance.* Your soul will be happy, and your joy will find outlets of adoring praise and vigorous industry.

5. A fervent spirit is one filled with the Spirit of God. When Jesus cried, "If any man thirst, let him come unto me and drink," and promised that rivers of living water should flow through the heart of the believer, "he spake of the Spirit, which they that believe on him should receive." The Holy Spirit is actually bestowed on the people of God. He is to them a better Spirit, restraining and superseding their own. He is the author of that athletic self-denial and flesh-conquering fervor of which they are conscious from time to time. It is he who gives such delight in drawing near

* Ps. xxx. 11, 12.

to God, that the believer at seasons could "pray and never cease;" and it is he who gives that transforming affection to the person of Christ, and that heroic ardor in the service of Christ, to which inactivity is irksome, and silence oppressive. And whosoever would enjoy the gentle manuduction which leads into all truth and all duty—whosoever would persevere in the placid discharge of allotted labor, and maintain amid it all a calm and thankful walk with God, must put himself at the disposal of this heavenly Visitant. The heart is "dry as summer's dust" from which the Spirit of God departs; and that is the believing, loving, happy, and energetic heart, in which the Holy Spirit dwells.

6. A fervent spirit is a prayerful spirit. The Holy Spirit is the New Testament gift most absolutely promised in answer to prayer*—and though, perhaps, the gift whose bestowment is least the matter of a lively consciousness to the recipient at the mo-

* Luke xi. 13. John xiv. 14, 16; xvi. 24.

ment, the gift from which, in the long-run of life, the largest and most important results are evolved, and the gift which, in the retrospect of eternity, the believer may find that he enjoyed more abundantly and more constantly than he himself ever imagined. As it is, there are times when the presence of this Almighty Comforter is easily realized. When the soul is lifted far above its natural selfishness, so that it can make vast sacrifices without any misgiving—when fortified against its natural timidity, so that it can face frightful perils without any trepidation—and when invigorated with such unwonted ardor as to forget its natural indolence, and not feel its inherent weakness, the soul can readily understand that this mighty strengthening inwardly is the work of the Holy Spirit. And it is this persuasion which brings the believer strength in weakness. Conscious of lethargy creeping over him—alarmed at the declension of his zeal, and the waning of his love—fearful to what his present apathy may grow, and remembering how different were the days of old—he breathes a prayer, at first faint and desponding, but still a prayer: "Wilt thou not revive us again? Awake, O north wind; come thou south." And, while he is yet speaking, he begins to revive. As if the clear weather were brightening the atmosphere, the great realities grow distinct and near. The things eternal are seen again, and the powers of the coming world are felt. His soul is restored. Or a great work is given him to do, and his strength is small. "O Lord, with thee is the fountain of life. Lord, pity me, for I am weak." And the Lord pities him, and sends forth his quickening Spirit; and the difficulty is surmounted, and the work is done: and, without so much as feeling the fire and water which lay between, he gains the wealthy place.

7. A fervent spirit is one which easily sunders a man from selfishness, and sloth, and other besetting sins. On a winter's day I have noticed a row of cottages, with a deep load of snow on their several roofs;

but, as the day wore on, large fragments began to tumble from the eaves of this one and that other, till, by-and-by, there was a simultaneous avalanche, and the whole heap slid over in powdery ruin on the pavement: and, before the sun went down, you saw each roof as clear and dry as on a summer's eve. But here and there you would observe one with its snow-mantle unbroken, and a ruff of stiff icicles round it. What made the difference? The difference was to be found within. Some of these huts were empty, or the lonely inhabitant cowered over a scanty fire; while the peopled hearth and the high-blazing fagots of the rest created such an inward warmth that grim winter relaxed his melting gripe, and the loosened mass folded off and tumbled over on the miry street. It is possible by some outside process to push the main volume of snow from the frosty roof, or chip off the icicles one by one. But they will form again, and it needs an inward heat to create a total thaw. And so, by sundry processes, you may clear off from a man's conduct the dead weight of conspicuous sins; but it needs a hidden heat, a vital warmth within, to produce such a separation between the soul and its besetting iniquities, that the whole wintry incubus, the entire body of sin, will come spontaneously away. That vital warmth is the love of God abundantly shed abroad—the kindly glow which the Comforter diffuses in the soul which he makes his home. His genial inhabitation thaws that soul and its favorite sins asunder, and makes the indolence, and self-indulgence, and indevotion, fall off from their old resting-place on that dissolving heart. The easiest form of self-mortification is a fervent spirit.

8. And a fervent spirit is the most abundant source of an active life. In heaven there is a perfect activity, because in heaven there is a perfect fervor. They are all happy there. They have a sufficient end in all they do. There is no wearying in their work, for there is no waning in their love.

The want of a sufficient object would make any man idle. A friend once found the author of "The Seasons" in bed long after noon; and upbraiding him for his indolence, the poet remarked that he just lay still because, although he were up, he would have nothing to do. But, even in this sluggish world, there are those whose hearty relish of their work and sense of its importance so inspire, that they are very loath when slumber constrains them to quit it, and often prevent the dawning in order to resume it. It was mathematical fervor which kept Newton poring on his problems till the midnight wind swept over his papers the ashes from his long-extinguished fire. It was artistic fervor which kept Reynolds with the pencil in his glowing hand for thirty-six hours together, evoking from the canvass forms of beauty that seemed glad to come. It was poetic fervor which sustained Dryden in a fortnight's phrensy, when composing his "Ode on St. Cecilia's Day," heedless of privations which he did not so much as perceive. And it was scientific fervor which dragged the lazy but eloquent French naturalist, Buffon, from beloved slumbers to his still more beloved studies, for many years together. There is no department of human distinction which can not record its feats of fervor. But shall science, with its corruptible crowns, and the world, with its vanities, monopolize this enthusiasm? If not, let each one consider, "What is the greatest self-denial to which a godly zeal has prompted me? Which is the largest or the greatest work through which a holy fervor has ever carried me?"*

* It would have been right, had there been room, to mention some things which are detrimental or fatal to fervor of spirit. 1. Guilt on the conscience. 2. Debt and worldly entanglements. 3. Sabbaths not sanctified. 4. Late and frequent visiting. 5. Indulgence in frivolous literature. 6. Restraining prayer. 7. A wrong theology.

LECTURE V.

THE THREEFOLD CORD.

"*Not slothful in business; fervent in spirit; serving the Lord.*"—ROMANS XII. 11.

WERE you ever struck with the sobriety of Scripture? There are many good thoughts in human compositions, and many hints of truth in human systems; but in proportion as they are original or striking, they border on extravagance. You can not follow them fully till you find yourself toppling on the verge of a paradox, or are obliged to halt in the midst of a glaring absurdity. There are many excellent ideas in the old philosophy, and some valuable principles in the ethics of later schools; but they all show, though it were in nothing but their *extremeness*, their frail original, their human infirmity their wrong-side bias. And so is it with many religious systems, built on insulated texts of Scripture. They are not without a basis of truth, but that basis is partial. The extremeness of religionism pounces on a single text, or a single class of texts, and walls them off from the rest of revelation, and cultivates them exclusively—bestows on them the irrigation of constant study, and reaps no harvests except those which grow on this favorite territory—and looks on all the rest of the Bible as a sort of common, an unenclosed waste, a territory good for little or nothing, except a short occasional excursion; ay, and perhaps frowns on another class of texts with a secret jealousy, as texts which had better never have been there—a dangerous group, whose creeping roots or wafted thistle-down threaten evil to the enclosure of their own favorite little system. If the texts so treated be doctrinal, the result of this partiality, this exclusiveness or extremeness, is *sectarianism ;* if the texts so treated be practical, the result is *religious singularity.* But sectarianism of doctrine and singularity of practice, whatever countenance they get from single clauses and detached sentences of Scripture, are contradicted and condemned the moment you confront them with a complete Bible. Hence it happens, that while there never was a doctrinal or practical error which had not some text to stand upon, there never was one which dared encounter openly and honestly the entire Word of God. In other words, there has seldom been an error which did not include some important truth ; but just as surely as it included some truth, so it excluded others. And just as oxygen alone will never make the atmosphere, or hydrogen alone will never make the ocean, or red beams alone will never make the sun, so one fact, or one set of ideas, will never make the truth. A truth, by abiding alone, becomes to all intents an error.

Nothing can be more different from the partiality of man than the completeness and comprehensiveness of Scripture. Nothing can be more opposite to man's extremeness than the sobriety of Scripture. It does not deal in hyperbole or paradox; it puts the truth, calmly, fully, and in all its goodly proportions. Unlike the systems of man's invention, its ethics do not flutter on the solitary wing of one only virtue, nor do they dot along on the uneven legs of a short theology and a longer morality. Its philanthropy does not consist in hating yourself, nor does its love to God require you to forget your brother. Its perfection of character is not pre-eminence in one particular, nor does it inculcate any excellence which requires the annihilation of all the rest. Though neither a see-saw of counterpoising virtues and vices, nor a neutral mixture of opposing elements, there is a balance of excellence, a blending of graces, in the gospel ideal of character. It forgets neither the man himself, nor the God above him, nor the world around him. It teaches us to live godly, but it does not forget to teach us to live righteously and soberly. It urges diligence in business, but it does not omit to enjoin fervor of spirit and devotedness to the Lord.

I do not know that we can select a more opportune exemplication of these contrary principles—the partiality of human religion and the comprehensiveness of scriptural religion—than the text with which you are now so familiar, and the treatment which its several precepts have received at the hands of men. I think it may be very easily shown that each separate clause has been the motto of a several sect, the watchword of a separate party: each right, so far as it remembered that special clause—each wrong, so far as it forgot the other two.

1. First, "Not slothful in business."—There have been in all ages those who were very willing to sum up religion in discharging the duties of their calling. If they were servants, they were conscious of great in-

dustry, and a real attention to their employers' interest. If wives or mothers, they were notable for keeping at home, and caring after their own concerns. They looked well to the ways of their household, and ate not the bread of idleness; and could the trim threshold and each tidy arrangement of the well-ordered dwelling tell the full tale of anxious thoughts, and early rising, and worrying bustle, which have been expended upon them, happy the empire which had such prime minister as rules this little realm. If men of business, they feel that they are busy men. They mind their own affairs, and do not interfere in other men's matters. They are at it late and early; the summer's sun does not seduce them from their dingy counting-room, nor do the amenities of literature bewitch them from the anxieties of money-making. They seldom treat themselves to a holyday, and, what is more to the purpose, they do not despatch business by halves; they work in good earnest. They feel as if the chief end of man lay somewhere about the terminus of their own trade or profession, and they push on accordingly. Then there mingles with it all a complacent feeling. "It is not for myself I thus tug and strain, and grow prematurely old: it is for others. 'He that provides not for his own house, hath denied the faith, and is worse than an infidel.'— 'If any man will not work, neither let him eat.' We are commanded to redeem the time, and are forbidden to be slothful in business." And if to this again should be superadded a certain amount of overt and ostensible religion—if this busy man or cumbered housekeeper should withal read a daily chapter, and maintain the regular form of family worship, and the equally regular form of churchgoing—above all, if his business should prosper, and nothing occur to vex his conscience, he is very apt to feel— "What lack I yet? True, I pretend to no peculiar sanctity; but I believe I am as honest, and industrious, and sober, as those who do. I may not get into the raptures into which some try to work themselves, nor do I fuss about from sermon to sermon and from meeting to meeting, as many do; but I believe my respect for religion is as real, and my intentions as good, as theirs. And though I do not lay the same stress on speculative points and matters of faith, no man can accuse me of neglecting the weightier matters of the law." Now the industrious element in this character is good, but if this be the whole of it, in the Bible balance it will be found deplorably wanting. A man may be all that you describe yourself, without being born again; he may be all this, and his heart never have been made right with God; and of all the work he has done so heartily, nothing may have been done as unto the Lord—in the animation of that love, and in the singleness of that loyalty, without which the most fagging toil is but an earnest self-idolatry. And he may be all this without any of that fervor of spirit which will make a man happy in that world where the things of our present faith are the visible sources of joy, and where psalm-singing and the other outpourings of ecstatic hearts are the exercises most congenial.

2. But then again—"fervent in spirit." Others have erred in subliming the whole of Christianity into fervor. They fancy that there is no outlet for piety except in emotion. They forget that the engine may be doing most work when none of the steam is blowing off; and therefore they are not content except they *feel* a great deal, and live in constant excitement. They forget that the best form that feeling can take is the practical form—the praying, praising, working form. Or if it should take this form, their fervor is ill-directed. It is not fairly distributed; they are fervent in secret or in the sanctuary, but not fervent in society; they are fervent in controversies, but not in truths conceded; they are fervent in the things of their own denomination, but not in the things of Jesus Christ; or if fervent in HIS cause, they fix on the fields of labor far away, and contemn those nearer home.

Their fervor is reserved for hallowed places and devotional hours, and does not pervade their daily life. They will rise from a prayer in which they have expatiated on the glory of the latter day—" Thy kingdom come, thy will be done on earth as it is in heaven," and some ordinary duty is awaiting them; they are asked to fulfil some prosaic service, to do some such matter-of-fact employment as angels in heaven are apt to do; and the sight of actual labor disperses their good frame in a moment. their praying fervor is not a working fervor. Or they have just been singing, under some extraordinary afflatus, a hymn about universal peace or millennial glory; but the unopened letter turns out to be a despatch from some villanous correspondent: or the moment the worship is over, some gross negligence or some provoking carelessness accosts them, and the instant explosion proves, that were they living in the millennium, there would be at least one exception to the universal peace. Or they have come back from some jubilant missionary meeting, where their hearts were really warm, where they loudly cheered the speeches, and where their ears tingled at the recital of some affecting instance of liberality; and they are hardly safe in their homes, when the ill-favored collector assails them, and they are asked for the solid sympathy of their substance. Yes—oh ignominy! oh bathos!—after they have given their tears, asked for their gold! And they feel as if it were a fatal transition, a most headlong climax, from delicious emotion down to vulgar money. And thus it is that they continue to let as much feeling vanish in inaction, as much fervor fly off in mere emotion, as, if turned on in the right direction, might have propelled some mighty enterprise, or conducted to a safe and joyful conclusion many a work of faith and labor of love.

3. "Serving the Lord." In Old-Testament times it was not unusual for persons of eminent piety to dedicate themselves entirely to temple-service, waiting on God in

prayer continually night and day. Thus Samuel was dedicated to the Lord all the days of his life: so we presume was the maid of Gilead, Jephthah's daughter: and so was Anna the prophetess, who departed not from the temple the eighty-four years of her long widowhood. In seeking this seclusion they were practically carrying out the psalmist's devout behest: "One thing have I desired of the Lord, that will I seek after; that I may dwell in the house of the Lord all the days of my life, to behold the beauty of the Lord and to inquire in his temple." And a pleasant life it were, away from a stormy world in the calm pavilion of God's own presence, and away from the tantalizing phantoms, vexing cares, and stunning noise of delirious mortality, to see no beauty less soul-filling than his own, and hear no voice less assuring than His who says, "My peace I give unto you." But the gospel dispensation is not the era of anchorets, and recluses, and temple-devotees; or, more properly speaking, every disciple of the Savior ought to be alike a devotee. He should live not to himself, but to Him who loved him. He should be a self-devoted, a dedicated man—a living sacrifice, but a sacrifice diffusing its sweet savor in the scenes of ordinary life, and regaling, not heaven alone, but earth, with its grateful exhalations. He should seek to behold his Lord's beauty and dwell in his Lord's presence all the days of his life; but now that neither Jerusulem nor Samaria is the temple, his believing heart should be the shrine, and his ascending Savior's promise—"Lo, I am with you"—sbould be the Shekinah. Wherever he goes, he should carry his Lord's presence along with him; and whatever he is doing, he should be doing his heavenly Master's work. However, this life of active devotedness does not suit the taste of many. In order to serve the Lord, they feel that they must leave the living world. They must off and away to some cleft of the rock, some lodge of the far wilderness, some—

> "sacred solitude,
> "Where Quiet with Religion makes her home."

To be diligent in business they feel incompatible with serving the Lord; and even that more hallowed business which is occupied with ministering to the bodies and souls of men is a rude break in their retirement, a jar in their contemplative joys. They would rather be excused from anything which forces them into contact with unwelcome flesh and blood, and reminds them of this selfish world and its gross materialism. Their closet is more attractive than the cottage of poverty; meditations of the rest which remaineth are more congenial than toils in the work of the day; and pensive lamentations over the world's wickedness come more spontaneous than real earnest efforts to make this bad world better. Now it is impossible to be too devoted, if that devotedness make you correspondingly fervent in spirit and diligent in business. You can not pray too much, though you should pray without ceasing, if your prayer take a practical direction, and lead you to do good without ceasing. But it is just as possible to run away from the Lord's service by running into retirement as by running into the world. In the retirement of the ship, and then in the completer retirement of the whale's belly, Jonah was as much a rebel and a runaway as in the noisy streets of Joppa. Had he wished to "serve the Lord," his "business" was to have been at Nineveh. And it little matters whether it be the recluse of the desert who absconds from his brethren, and leaves the sick to tend themselves, and the ignorant to teach themselves, and the careless to convert themselves—or the recluse of the closet, who leaves the neglected household to take care of itself, the slipshod children to look after themselves, and the broken furniture to mend itself: each in his own way is slothful in business, under a self-deceiving pretext that he is serving the Lord.

Thus you perceive that each of the three classes—the mere bustlers, the mere feelers, and the mere devotees—by being right in only one thing, are altogether wrong. These are not fancy sketches, nor are they studies from the antique. True, you may find the counterpart of the first class in the correct morality and heartless formalism of that worldly professorship, that "Whole Duty of Man" pharisaism which once abounded in these very lands. And you may represent the second by that fifth-monarchy fervor, that unproductive zeal, which has marked some periods of the church, which possibly marks some sections still. And you will find the third exemplified in all the mystic devotion and day-dreaming quietism of world-weary recluses, popish and protestant, in every age. Though all can quote one fragment of this text, all are wrong, by not being able to quote the whole. Those who are diligent in business, but in that business do not serve the Lord, their selfish diligence is but a busy idleness, a hypocritical activity. Their time-bounded and self-reverting work is the ineffectual labor of the convict who digs the pit and fills it up again—who draws water from the well and pours it back again. And so the devotedness which results in no diligence is like the planning of a house which is never built, the daily purposing of a journey which is never set about. The fervor of spirit which, withal, is slothful in business, is like the stream falling on the mill-wheel, but the connecting shaft is broken—and though the wheel turns nimbly round, the detached machinery stands still, and no work is done ; or like the disconnected engine and tender, which bolt away by themselves, and leave the helpless train still standing where it stood.

Now in opposition to all these defective versions, these maimed and truncated representations, this verse delineates the Christian character in its completeness, hard-working, warmly-feeling, single-eyed, "not slothful in business"—"fervent in spirit"—"serving the Lord." And if you look at the Christian philosophy of the subject, you will find that it is the single eye which awakes the fervent spirit, and the fervent spirit which sets the busy hands and feet in willing motion.

1. It is an eye fixed on Jesus which kindles the fervent spirit. An unconverted man is not happy. There is a dull load on his spirit—a dim cloud on his conscience—he scarcely knows what he would be at—but he certainly is not happy. If a considerate man, he is aware that there must be a joy in existence which he has not yet struck out—a secret of more solid bliss which he hitherto has not hit upon. He is not at peace with God. He has not secured an explicit reconciliation with his Creator and Sovereign. God's frown is upon him—a frown as wide as is the sinner's universe. Go where he may, he can not get out into the clear daylight of a glad conscience and a propitious heaven. And it is not till he finds his way into the Goshen of the gospel, the sun-lit region on which the beams of God's countenance still smile down, through the doorway by which an ascending Savior

entered heaven—it is not till, from the gross darkness and palpable gloom of a natural condition, a man is led into the grateful light and glorious liberty of the sons of God—it is not till then that he knows the ecstasy of undiluted joy and the perfection of that peace which passeth all understanding. It is not till the Spirit of adoption makes him a child of God that he thoroughly feels himself a man; and it is in the sweet sense of forgiveness, and in the transporting assurance that he is now on the same side with Omnipotence, that he first breathes freely. The thrill of a sudden animation sweeps through all his frame; and, encountering an unwonted gayety all around him, he perceives an unwonted energy within him. Peace with God has brought him power from God, and with the Lord he loves to dictate, there is no work which he is loath to do; and with that Lord upon his side, none which he can not hope to do. The convict-labor and hireling-tasks of the alien and bondsman are exchanged for the free-will offerings and affectionate services of a son and a disciple. Reconciled to God, he is reconciled to everything which comes from God; and full of the love of Christ, he courts everything which he can do for Christ. "Come, labor, for I rather love thee now. Come, hard work and long work, I am in a mood for you now. Come, trials and crosses, for I can carry you now. Come, death, for I am ready for thee now." His relation to Christ has put him in a new relation to everything else; and the same fountain which has washed the stain from his conscience having washed the scales from his eyes, an inundation of light and of beauty bursts in from the creation around him, which hitherto was to him as much an unknown universe as its Creator was the unknown God; and the boundless inflowings of peaceful images, and happy impressions, and strong consolations, dilate his soul with an elasticity, an enterprise, and courage, as new as they are divine. He has found a Savior, and his soul is happy. The Lord

Jesus is his friend; and his spirit, once so frigid, is become a fervent spirit. His new views have made him a new man.

2. The fervent spirit creates the industrious life. Sulky labor and the labor of sorrow are little worth. Whatever a man does with a guilty feeling, he is apt to do wrong; and whatever he does with a melancholy feeling, he is likely to do by halves. Look to that little boy sitting down to his hated lesson after a burst of passion. Do you notice how long the same page lies open before the pouting student, and how solemnly he watches the blue-bottle raging round the room and bouncing against the window? Look at his blurred copy-book, its trembling strokes and blotted loops a memento of this angry morning. And the sum upon the slate, only here and there a figure right, an emblem of his rebellious mind, all at sixes and sevens with itself. It is *guilt* that makes him a trifler. It is *guilt* that makes him blunder. *Guilt* makes him wretched; and therefore all he does is

wrong. But sometimes grief disables or disinclines for exertion as much as guilt. You may remember times when such a sorrow possessed you, that you not only forgot to eat your daily bread, but had no heart to do your daily work. You did not care to set your house in order, for some stunning intelligence or fearful foreboding had paralyzed all your energy. You did not care to hear your children's tasks, for the shadows of yon sick-room had diffused a look of orphanage on them and on everything. And the more delightsome the recreation once had been, the more congenial the labor, so much the deeper was the funereal die it had now imbibed, and the more did your heart revolt from it. Sorrow makes the eyes heavy, even when they can not sleep; and, for inefficiency, next to the blundering work of a guilty conscience, is the dull work of a weary or wounded spirit. If you could only shed tranquillity over the conscience, and infuse joy into the soul, you would do more to make the man a thorough worker than if you could lend him the force of Hercules or the hundred arms of Briareus. Now, the gospel, freely admitted, makes the man happy. It gives him peace *with* God and makes him happy *in* God. Its strong consolation neutralizes the sting of reluctant labor and the curse of penal toil. Its advent of heavenly energy takes the languor out of life, and much of its inherent indolence out of lazy human nature. It chases spectres from the fancy and lions from the street. It gives industry a noble look which selfish drudgery never wore; and from the moment that a man begins to do his work for his Savior's sake, he feels that the most ordinary works are full of sweetness and dignity, and that the most difficult are not impossible. "Through Christ strengthening me, I can do all things." And if any one of you, my friends, is weary with his work—if dissatisfaction with yourself, or sorrow of any kind, disheartens you—if, at any time, you feel the dull paralysis of conscious sin, or the depressing influence of vexing thoughts—look to Jesus and be happy. Be happy, and go to work.

LECTURE VI.

A WORD TO EACH AND TO ALL—CONCLUSION.

"*Not slothful in business; fervent in spirit; serving the Lord.*"—ROMANS XII. 11.

CHRISTIAN industry is just the outlet of a fervent spirit, a Christ-devoted heart. The industry which is not fervent is not Christian, and on the other hand, the love which does not come out in action, the fervor which does not lead to diligence, will soon die down. He who has an eye to Christ in all he does, and whose spirit is full of that energy, that love to his work and his brethren, and his Master in heaven, which the Holy Spirit gives, will not soon weary in well-doing.

1. Some of you are SERVANTS. Some of you are in families where there is no fear of God, and some of you serve employers who take no interest in you, who, however hard you toil, and however well you do your work, never thank you nor notice your exertions. This is discouraging; but before you entered that family, had you not entered the service of the Lord Jesus Christ? and when you came to this new place you surely did not leave this higher and nobler service. Very true, the individual from whom you receive your immediate orders may be very unreasonable, and exceedingly unamiable, and the thanks you get may be sorry remuneration for your conscientious industry. But have you not a Master in heaven, whose eye is always upon you, who takes interested note of all you do, and who, whatever you do in secret for *his* sake, will reward you openly? You do not mean to say that all your

end in working is to get so much wages, with a kind word or a look of approval now and then. If you carry the spirit of discipleship into your every-day duties, you will find that there is a way to make the meanest occupation honorable and the most irksome employment easy. Work which you do for the Lord's sake, will never be wearisome, and however little man may notice or acknowledge it, your labor in the Lord will never be vain. And I know not if there be any department of life where there is more abundant room for a truly Christian ambition than the calling which you occupy. Whether like Eliezer of Damascus, you serve a Father of the Faithful, or like Joseph and the Israelitish maid, be in the household of a pagan or a worldling; you have singular opportunities for adorning the doctrine of your God and Savior. Good man as Abraham was, and good man as Eliezer was, there was once a time when Abraham, in a tone of evident disappointment, said, " Behold, to me thou hast given no seed, and lo, one born in my house is mine heir." But so completely had the consistent kindness and fidelity of Eliezer won the affection of his chief, that at the last Abraham could scarcely have wished a better heir than his servant, or Eliezer found a more indulgent father than his master. Joseph had no motive for serving Pharoah, except that anxiety to fulfil an important office well, and that hearty love of labor which distinguish men of a healthy mind and conscientious spirit. But such a zealous charge did he take of Pharoah's interests, so intelligently and sleeplessly did his eye travel through the realm, that Egypt wore another aspect under Joseph's rule, and its revenues became as rich as a provident and benignant administration could make them. The little maid of Israel was a captive, and if the joy of the Lord had not been her strength, she would have had no spirit to work. She would have pined after her home among the hills of Samaria, and when she thought of the pleasant cottage from which fierce ruffians had torn her away, and named over to herself, one by one, the playfellows whom she would never see again, she would have broken her young heart and sat down in sulky silence, or perhaps have died. But she loved the Lord God of Israel; and as he had sent her to Damascus and into the house of a heathen lady, she made up her mind and set to work right earnestly, and soon got on to take a real interest in her new abode. She loved her mistress and was sorry for the deplorable sufferings of her afflicted lord, and suggested the visit to Elisha which resulted in his wondrous cure. And both Joseph and the little maid, by serving the Lord with a fervent spirit, not only made their own life pass pleasantly in a foreign land, but they made a great impression on those around them. Joseph's God was magnified in the eyes of Pharoah, and the little maid soon saw Naaman a worshipper of the true Jehovah. And you who are in the service of others, seek to serve the

Lord. Perhaps like Joseph and the little maid you are far from home. Perhaps like them you are doing work for those in whom you had no interest formerly, and who even now have not the fear of God before them. But your Lord paramount is the Lord Jesus himself; the real Master who has sent you here and given you this uphill work to do is Christ; and if you only set about it for his sake, with a happy, interested, resolute mind, your work will grow every day easier; your conscience will sing; the light of the Lord's presence will gild the dim passages and stranger-looking chambers of your place of sojourn; your character will ere long commend itself, and better still, may commend your Master in Heaven. "For he that in these things serveth Christ is acceptable to God, and approved of men."

2. Some of you are SCHOLARS either receiving the education which fits for ordinary life, or which may qualify you for some particular profession. Here too you have

need of industry. I hope you love learning for its own sake; I hope you love it still more for the Lord's sake. The more things you know, and the more things you can do, the more respected, and consequently, the more influential and useful will you hereafter be. If you grow up an ignorant man few will care for your company. People will be laughing at your mistakes and your blunders. And even if you should be wishful to do good, you will scarcely know how to set about it. The usefulness and happiness of your future life depend very much on the amount of solid learning and graceful accomplishments, and above all, on the extent of bible knowledge which you presently acquire, and if you be only willing you may acquire as much as ever you please. To use the words of the most philosophic of British Artists, "Nothing is denied to well-directed diligence." Long ago, a little boy was entered at Harrow School. He was put into a class beyond his years, and where all the scholars had the advantage of previous instruction denied to him. His master chid him for his dulness, and all his own efforts could not raise him from the lowest place on the form. But, nothing daunted, he procured the grammars and other elementary books which his class-fellows had gone through in previous terms. He devoted the hours of play, and not a few of the hours of sleep, to the mastering of these ; till in a few weeks he gradually began to rise, and it was not long till he shot far a-head of all his companions, and became not only dux of that division but the pride of Harrow. That boy, whose career began with this fit of energetic application, you may see his statue in St. Paul's cathedral to-morrow ; for he lived to be the greatest oriental scholar of modern Europe, and most of you have heard the name of Sir William Jones. God denies nothing in the way of learning to well-directed diligence. It is possible that you may be rather depressed than stimulated when asked to contemplate some first-rate name in literature or science. When you see the lofty pinnacle of attainment on which that name is now reposing, you fee as if it had been created there rather than had travelled thither. No such thing. The most illustrious in the annals of philosophy, once on a time, knew no more of it than you now do. And how did he arrive at his peerless proficiency? By dint of diligence, by downright painstaking. When Newton was asked how he came by those discoveries which looked like divination or intuitions of a higher intelligence rather than the results of mere research, he declared that he could not otherwise account for them unless it were that he could pay longer attention to the subject than most men cared to do. In other words, it was by diligence in his business that he became the most renowned of British sages. The discovery of gravitation, the grand secret of the universe, was not whispered in his ear by any oracle. It did not drop into his idle lap a windfall from the clouds. But he reached it by self-denying toil, by midnight study, by the large command of accurate science, and by bending all his powers of mind in the one direction, and keeping them thus bent. And whatever may be the subject of your pursuit, if you have any natural aptitude for it at all, there is no limit to your proficiency except the limits of your own pains-taking. There is no wishing-cap which will fetch you knowledge from the east or west. It is not likely to visit you in a morning dream, nor will it drop through your study roof into your elbow chair. It is not a lucky advent which will alight on your loitering path some twilight, like Minerva's owl, and create you an orator, an artist, or a scholar on the spot. It is an ultimatum which you must make up your mind that it is worth your while attaining; and trudge on steadily toward it, and not count that day's work hard, nor that night-watching long, which advances you one step toward it, or brings its welcoming beacon one bright hope nearer.

3. Some of you are TEACHERS. It is much to be lamented that there are so few enthusiasts in this honorable and important work. Many who are engaged in it regard it as a bondage, and sigh for the day which shall finally release them from its drudgery and din. They have never felt that theirs is a high calling, nor do they ever enter the school-room with the inspiring consciousness, that they go as missionaries and pastors there. They undervalue their scholars. Instead of regarding them as all that now exists of a generation as important as our own; instead of recognising in their present dispositions the mischief or beneficence which must tell on wide neighborhoods ere a few short years are run; instead of training up immortal spirits and expansive minds for usefulness now and glory afterward, many teachers have never seen their pupils in any other light than as so many rows of turbulent rebels, a rabble of necessary torments, a roomful of that mighty plague of which the Nile of our

noisy humanity is all croaking and jumping over. And many undervalue themselves. Instead of recollecting their glorious vocation, and eying the cloud of teacher-witnesses with whom they are encompassed; instead of a high-souled zeal for their profession, as that which should form the plastic mind after the finest models of human attainment and scriptural excellence, many regard their office as so menial that they have always the feeling as if themselves were pedants. To prescribe the task, to hear the lesson, to administer monotonous praise and blame, is the listless round of their official perfunctoriness. But there are few fields of brighter promise than the calling of a teacher. If he give himself wholly to it, if he set before him the highest object of all tuition, the bringing souls to Christ; if he can form a real affection for his scholars, and maintain a parental anxiety for their proficiency and their principles; if he has wisdom enough to understand them, and kindness enough to sympathize with them;

if he has sufficient love for learning to have no distaste for lessons, he will be sure to inspire a zeal for study into the minds of many, he will win the love of all except the very few whose hearts are deaf-born, and in a short time the best features of his own character will be multiplying in spheres far-sundered in the kindred persons of grateful pupils. Should he live long enough, they will praise him in the gate of public life, or cheer his declining days in the homes which he taught them to make happy. Or should he die soon enough, the rest from his labors will ever and anon be heightened by the arrival of another and another of the children whom God hath given him.

But without descending to more minute particulars, let me remind you, my friends, that all of you who are members of this church have got a special "business" as the professed disciples of Jesus Christ. In the day when Christ said to you, "Arise, follow me,' he called you to a life like his own, a life of industry and self-denial, and continual doing good. You are a consistent Christian in proportion as you resemble him whose fervent spirit poured out not more in his midnight prayers than in his daily deeds of mercy, and who, whether he disputed with the doctors in the Temple, or conversed with the ignorant stranger at the well, or fed the five thousand with miraculous loaves, or summoned Lazarus from the tomb, was still about his Father's "business." They little understand the Christian life, who fancy that a slothful or languid profession will secure an abundant entrance into the heavenly kingdom. If the believer's progress from the cross to the crown be, as it is again and again represented, a race, a wrestling, a warfare, a fight, a continual watching, and a constant violence, there is good reason for the exhortations, "give *diligence* to make your calling and election sure. We desire that every one of you do show *diligence* to the full assurance of hope unto the end; that ye be *not slothful*, but followers of them who through faith and patience inherit the promises. Wherefore, brethren, seeing that you look for such things, be *diligent* that you may be found of him in peace, without spot and blameless."

It needs diligence to keep the conscience clean. "Herein do I exercise myself, to have always a conscience void of offence toward God and toward men." It needs diligence to keep up a happy hopefulness of spirit. "Gird up the loins of your mind, be sober, and hope to the end." It needs diligence to maintain a serene and strenuous orthodoxy. "Watch ye; stand fast in the faith; quit you like men; be strong." It needs diligence to maintain a blameless life. "Ye have not yet resisted unto blood, striving against sin." It needs diligence to lead a life conspicuously useful and God-glorifying. "Seeing we are compassed about with so great a cloud of witnesses (as Abel, and Enoch, and Noah, and Abraham, and Moses), let us lay aside every weight, and the sin which doth so easily beset us, and let us run with patience the race that is set before us, looking unto Jesus." And it needs diligence to attain a joyful welcome from Jesus and a full reward. "And besides this, giving all diligence, add to your faith, virtue [fortitude]; and to fortitude, knowledge; and to knowledge, temperance; and to temperance, patience; and to patience, godliness; and to godliness, brotherly-kindness; and to brotherly kindness, charity. Wherefore the rather, brethren, give diligence to make your calling and election sure; for if ye do these things [fortitude, &c.] ye shall never fall: for so an entrance shall be ministered unto you abundantly into the everlasting kingdom of our God and Savior Jesus Christ."—"And I heard a voice from heaven saying unto me, Write, Blessed are the dead which die in the Lord from henceforth; yea, saith the Spirit, that they may rest from their labors, and their works do follow them."—"Let us labor, therefore, to enter into that rest."*

To labor in the word and doctrine is the business of one; to feed the flock of God and rule the church of Christ is the business of others; to "serve tables," to care for and comfort the poor, and see that all things be done decently and in order, is the business of yet others; to teach the young and instruct the ignorant is the business of some; and to train up their households in the nurture and admonition of the Lord is the business of others; to obey their parents and to grow in wisdom—in favor with God and man—is the business of many; and to do work for others, with a willing hand and a single eye, is the business of many more. The work of the day needs diligence: much more does the work of eternity. It needs fervent diligence to be constantly serving our fellows; and it needs no less diligence to be directly serving Christ. To tend the sick, to visit the widows and fatherless in

* 2 Pet. i. 5–7, 10, 11. Rev. xiv. 13. Heb. iv. 11.

their affliction, to frequent the abodes of insulated wretchedness or congregated depravity, to set on foot schemes of Christian benevolence, and, still more, to keep them going—all this needs diligence. To put earnestness into secret prayer; to offer petitions so emphatic and express, that they are remembered afterward, and the answer watched for and expected; to commune with one's own heart, so as to attain some real self-acquaintance; to get into that humble, contrite, confessing frame, where the soul feels it sweet to lie beneath the cross, and "a debtor to mercy alone, of covenant mercy to sing;" to stir up one's soul to a thankful praising pitch; to beat down murmuring thoughts and drive vexing thoughts away; to get assurance regarding the foundations of the faith, and clear views of the truth itself; to have a prompt and secure command of Scripture; to possess a large acquaintance with the great salvation, and a minute acquaintance with all the details of Christian duty—all this needs no less diligence on our part, because God must give it or we shall never show it. To put life into family worship; to make it more than a duteous routine; to make its brief episode of praise, and prayer, and bible-reading, a refreshful ordinance, and influential on the day; to give a salutary direction to social intercourse, and season with timely salt the conversation of the friendly circle; to drive that "torpid ass,"* the body, to scenes of duty difficult and long-adjourned; to make a real business of public worship; to scowl away all pretexts for forsaking the solemn assembly; to spirit the reluctant flesh into a punctual arrival at the house of prayer, and then to stir up the soul to a cordial participation in all its services; to accompany with alert and affectionate eyes the reading of God's word, and listen with wakeful ear to the exposition and application of its lively oracles; to contribute a tuneful voice and a singing heart to our New-Testament offering of praise, and to put the whole stress

* Calvin *in loco.*

of an intelligent, and sympathizing, and believing earnestness into the supplications of the sanctuary, so that each petition shall ascend to the throne of grace with the deliberate signature of our Amen—all this requires a diligence, none the less because unless God work it in us, we shall never of ourselves muster up sufficient fervor thus to serve the Lord.

Dear brethren and Christian friends, consider what I say. There is little time to apply it; but you have heard from this text some hints of important truth—apply them for yourselves. As reasons why we desire to see a church more industrious and not less fervent and unworldly than the church has usually been, and as motives why each right-hearted man among you should this night start afresh on a career of busy devotedness and fervent industry, let me remind you—

1. Herein is the Father glorified, that ye bear much fruit.

2. Herein will you truly resemble, and

in measure re-exhibit the character of your blessed Lord and Master.

3. Hereby will yourselves be made far happier.

4. Hereby will the world be the better for your sojourn in it.

5. Hereby will the sadness of your departure be exceedingly alleviated.

6. And hereby will your everlasting joy be unspeakably enhanced.

Forbearing to dwell on these different considerations, let me revert for a little to the latter two.

A life of diligence and holy fervor prepares the believer for a peaceful departure. "Father, I have finished the work which thou gavest me to do; and now I come to thee." It was with unspeakable satisfaction that the Savior contemplated his return to the Father's bosom; and the reason was, because he knew so well that he had finished his Father's business. He could look back on the weary days and sleepless nights of his ministry, on the long years of his incarnation; and he saw that there was no righteousness which he had not fulfilled, no precept of the holy law which he had not magnified. His memory could not recall an idle word or a wasted hour; and even from the solemn twilight of Gethsemane his eye could trace serenely back the whole expanse of his earthly history, and see not one word which he would wish to recall, not one act which he could desire to alter; no sermon which, if he had to preach it over again, he would make more plain or more importunate; no miracle which, if it had to be performed afresh, he would do in a more impressive or effectual manner. He knew that there was no omission, no defect, and though the whole were to be done anew, he felt that the words could not be more gracious, nor the works more wonderful, than they had actually been. "Father, I have glorified thee on earth. I have finished the work which thou gavest me to do; and now I come to thee." The Lord Jesus was the first and the last who was ever able to say this; but through his strength made perfect in their weakness, some have made a nearer approach to this blessedness than their more remiss and indolent brethren. It was the grief of the pagan emperor Titus, when a day transpired in which he had learned no knowledge or done no good—"I have lost a day!" And—

> "'Tis a mournful story
> Thus in the ear of pensive eve to tell
> Of morning's firm resolves the vanished glory,
> Hope's honey left within the with'ring bell,
> And plants of mercy dead, that might have bloomed so well!"*

But it is a far more mournful story when the eve of life arrives, to be constrained to sigh, "I have lost a lifetime!"—"God gave me one lifetime, and it was once in my power to spend it as Aquila and Priscilla spent theirs—as Paul spent his—as Phebe spent hers. But now, that only life is closing, and, wo's me! how have I bestowed it? In making pin-cushions and playing the piano

* Mrs. Sigourney.

—in paying morning calls and evening visits."—"And *I*?—I have spent it in reading newspapers and novels—in dancing and singing songs, and telling diverting stories." —"And *I* have spent it in drinking and smoking—in games of cards and billiards—in frequenting taverns and theatres—in reading coarse tales and books of blasphemy." Yes: and though you should not need to look back on a life thus sinfully spent, it will be sad enough to review a life let idly slip. To think that by a right starting and a persevering continuance in well-doing, it was once in your power to have proved the large and permanent benefactor of your generation—to think that had you only begun with the Lord and held on in fervor of spirit, you might by this time have finished works which would make many bless your memory, and planted seeds of which hundreds would reap the pleasant fruits when yourself were in the clay; and then to remember that once on a time you had it in contemplation—it was all planned out and resolved upon, and day-dreamed over and over, but never resolutely gone about—to recollect "the morning's firm resolves" and sunny purposes, and then look at—

> "the vanished glory,
> Hope's honey left within the with'ring bell,
> And plants of mercy dead, that might have bloomed so well"—

how dreary it will make your deathbed, if capable of deliberate reflection then! How disconsolate it will render the retrospective evening of your days should you reach old age! And how different it will make your exit from his, who, looking back on his eventful career, could say, "I am now ready to be offered, and the time of my departure is at hand. I have fought a good fight, I have finished my course, I have kept the faith. Henceforth there is laid up for me a crown of righteousness, which the Lord, the righteous judge, shall give me at that day."

A life of Christian diligence is followed by an abundant entrance and a full reward.

There are two principles deep-seated in our nature: philosophy has got no name for them, but the Bible has an eye to each of them, and the gospel speaks to both of them. The possessions which we chiefly prize are either those which we have earned by our own industry, or gifts we have got from those we truly love. Perhaps there is some little slide in your desk, some secret drawer in your cabinet, which you do not often open—but when on a quiet holy-day you pull it gently out and look leisurely at it, your eye fills with tears. You read the date on the faded book-marker with a pensive smile, or you press the little picture to your lips and drop upon your knees, to pray for him whose image that little picture is. But a hard-visaged stranger peering over your shoulder might marvel what all this emotion meant; for he would not give a few shillings for the whole collection, and would think it liker the thing to be affected by the bunch of bank-notes, and bills, and government-securities, in the adjacent locker. And why do you prize it so? That picture was a keepsake from your brother when he crossed the Indian main ten summers since; that broidered riband is the only relic of the sister's love, who made you many a like remembrance, but whose mouldering fingers will make no more. Love lingers in these relics, and that is the reason why, when you stuff the bank-notes in your pocket, you clasp these trifles to your heart. Far more, if the gift or the bequest be one of vast intrinsic value. The estate, the house, the lands, which a fatherly kinsman or a dear friend conveyed to you—you prize them infinitely more than if they had come to you in the course of nature or by the laws of ordinary succession. You delight to show people over these grounds; and when they ask how long they have been in your family, your voice falters when you tell how they came to be yours. Sometimes when you look over the pastures and cornfields, the water tingles in your eye; for you feel that you are looking not at vulgar roods and common enclosures, but are gazing on acres of affection, on an expanse of unaccountable kindness. You commemorate the unusual gift by the giver's name. By some adjective of gratitude you connect it with his dear memory; and much as you may value it for its intrinsic worth, it is more precious still for the beloved donor's sake.

Then next to the possessions round which there hovers some symbol of living affection or departed kindness, we prize those possessions in which we recognise the fruits of our own diligence, the purchase of our own pains-taking. Next to the keepsakes of friendship, we delight in the rewards of personal industry. What a bright coin was that first sovereign which your own diligence ever earned! How solid and weighty did it feel! How fair did the monarch's image and superscription shine on its fresh-minted face, and how endless did its capabilities appear! Was there anything which that wonderful coin could not accomplish, any object of desire which it could not purchase? And wherefore such overweening affection for that one golden piece, for had you not possessed from time to time pocket-money of your own before? Yes—but it came too easily; it wanted the pleasant zest of industry; it did not bring into your bosom, as this one does, a whole freight of happy recollections, frugal hours, and self-denying labors, condensed into one solid equivalent, one tangible memento. What are the books in your library which you chiefly prize? Next to the gift-bible which solemnized the first birthday when you could read it; next to the book which your dying friend lifted from his pillow, and with your name tremulously inscribed, handed you on your last visit, when he had strength to do it; are they not the books which rewarded your blushing proficiency at the village-school, or commemorated your nightly labors in the first and happiest years of college-life, or those which your long-hoarded savings first enabled you to purchase? Why do you look with a kindlier eye on that juvenile literature than on the long rows of glittering learning and august philosophy which fill your crowded shelves? Why, but because there is something of a pleasant *personal* peculiar to them? The light of early days and industrious hours still floats around them. They are the sunny sepulchre in which much of your former self lies pleasantly embalmed, ready to start into a mellower life the moment memory bids it. Or why—to take the case already supposed, the opulent possessor of estates, which the love of another gave him—why is it that in the midst of luxuries and accommodations as abundant as wealth can purchase or ingenuity suggest—why is it that fruit from trees of his own planting, or from a garden of his own tending, tastes so sweet? Why is it that the rustic chair of his own contriving, or the telescope of his own constructing, so far surpasses any which the craftsman can send him? Why, the reason is, those apples have an aroma of industry, a smack of self-requiting diligence peculiar to themselves. That rustic seat is lined with self-complacent labor, and the pleasant consciousness of having made that telescope himself has so sharpened the maker's eye, as greatly to augment its magnifying power. God has so made the mind of man, that a peculiar deliciousness resides in the fruits of personal industry.

I repeat that the possessions which we chiefly prize—those of which the heart keeps the most tender yet tenacious hold—are not the windfalls of fortune, nor the heir-looms of regular succession, but the gifts of affection and the fruits of pains-taking; those in which something of ourself, or a dearer than ourself, still lives, and speaks, and feels. Now in regard to the supreme possession, the inheritance of heaven, the God of Love has consulted both of those deep-seated principles of the human soul. The heaven itself, the passport through its gates, and the right to its joys, are the purchase and the gift of Another. Nor is it to the believer the least enhancing element in its priceless possession that it is entirely the donation and bequest of his dearest friend. Looking forward to the pearly gates and golden streets of the celestial city, its love-built mansions and its life-watered paradise, the believer in Jesus delights to remember that they are purely the purchase, and as purely the gift of Immanuel. To think that he shall yet have his happy home on that Mount Zion; that with feet no longer sin-defiled he shall tread its radiant pavement and stand on its glassy sea; that with fingers no longer awkward he shall tell the harps of heaven what once he was and who made him what he is; that with a voice no longer trembling he shall transmit along the echoes of eternity the song of Moses and the Lamb; that his shall yet be a brow on which the drops of toil will never burst, and an eye which tears will never dim; that he himself shall wear a form that years shall never bend, and a countenance which grief can never mar; that his shall yet be a character on which the stains of time will leave no trace, and his a conscience pure enough to reflect the full image of Him who sits upon the throne—the thought of all this is amazement, ecstasy. But there is one thought more which puts the crown upon this blessedness—the climax on this joy :—

"These glorious hopes we owe to Jesus' dying love."

The name of this fair inheritance—Free Grace, God is love, Jehovah-Tsidkenu—identifies it with that name which the believer loves beyond all others. Heaven is doubly dear, as the heritage purchased for him by his Divine Redeemer; and all its glory is so heightened and solemnized, when he connects it with that adorable Friend who acquired it for him and conveys it to him, that though another heaven were in his offer, that other he would not accept. That heaven to which Immanuel is the living way—on whose earthward entrance atoning blood is sprinkled, on whose many mansions and amaranth crowns are the symbols which connect them with Calvary, and amid all whose countless joys the river of deepest pleasure is the love of Jesus—this is the only heaven to which the believer expects an entrance, and is the one of which his intensest longings say, "Would God that I were there!"

But even in this purchased possession there are ingredients of delight of an origin more personal to the believer himself—details of special blessedness, for the germe of which he must go back to his own earthly history; and just as the sweetest surprisals here below are those in which some effort of benevolence long bygone reverts upon you in its happy results—when you meet a stranger, and are charmed with his Christian intelligence and spiritual congeniality, and lo! it turns out that his religious history dates from a casual conversation with yourself in the guest-chamber or the public conveyance; or when you take refuge from the storm in a wayside cottage, and surveying with eager interest its arrangements of unwonted comfort and tastefulness, or listening to the bible-lesson of its little children fresh from school, mysterious hints of some similar yet different scene steal in upon your memory, till you begin to think, "I have surely been here before;" and anon the full truth flashes out: you have been there before, when it was a very different scene—when a drunken husband, and ragged children, and broken furniture, aroused your desponding commiseration; but the tract which you that day left has introduced sobriety, and a sabbath, and a family-bible, into that abject home, and made it what your grateful eyes now see—so the sweetest surprisals of eternity will be similar resurrections of the works of time. When the disciple has forgotten the labor of love, he will be reminded of it in the rich reward; and though he never thought any more of the cup of cold water which he gave, or the word in season which he spake in Jesus's name—though he made no memorandum of the visits of mercy which he paid, or the asylums which he found for the orphan and the outcast—it seems that they are registered in the book of remembrance, and will all be read by their happy author in the reviving light of glory.* To find the marvellous results which have accrued from feeble means—to encounter higher in salvation than yourself those of whose salvation you scarcely ever noped to hear, and learn that an entreaty, or prayer, or forgotten effort of your own, had a divine bearing on the joyful consummation—to find the prosperous fruit already growing on the shores of eternity from seeds which you scattered on the streams of time—with what discoveries of unexpected delight it will variegate the joys of the purchased possession, and with what accessions of adoration and praise it will augment the exceeding weight of glory! Oh brethren! strive to obtain an abundant entrance and a full reward. Seek to be so useful, that the world will miss you when away: or whether this world miss you or not, that in a better world there may be

* Dan. xii. 3; Matt. xxv. 34–40; Matt. x. 42.

many to welcome you as you enter it, and many to follow you when you have long been there. And above all, so live for Christ, so travail in his service, that when you fall asleep, a voice may be heard from heaven, saying, "Blessed are the dead which die IN THE LORD: yea, saith the Spirit, that they may rest from their LABORS, and their WORKS do follow them."

THE END.

www.ingramcontent.com/pod-product-compliance
Lightning Source LLC
LaVergne TN
LVHW021358110826
845150LV00007B/1702

* 9 7 8 1 4 2 5 5 1 3 9 6 2 *